Development of Educational System in India

(A Source Book for Teacher Educators and Teachers-in-Training)

Prof. A.S. Thakur
B.A., M.A. (Panjab); B-Ed. (Delhi);
M-Ed. (Durham); Ph-D. (A.B.U.)

Dr. Sandeep Berwal
B.Sc., M.Sc., M-Ed., Ph-D. (Kurukshetra);
D.I.R. (University Gold Medalist);
S.L.E.T. (Education) J&K and Gujarat;
U.G.C. - N.E.T. (Education)

SHIPRA

(2015, First Published in 2008)

Rs. 750, US$ 25

ISBN: 978-81-7541-425-9

2023 Impression

Development of Education System in India

Published by:
SHIPRA PUBLICATIONS
LG 18-19, Pankaj Central Market,
I.P. Ext., Patparganj, Delhi 110092
+ 91 11 22235152/ 6152; 9650028065
info@shiprapublication.com
www.shiprapublication.com

Contents

Section–II
COLONIAL PERIOD
(*Hide and Seek*)

Section–IV
Modern Developments
(Facing Realities)

Preface

The book titled *Development of Educational System in India* is a source book for B.Ed., M.Ed., and M.Phil., courses of universities in India. In it, an attempt has been made to recapitulate our past, analyse the present and indicate trends for the future.

The important facts of history in the development of educational system from the remote past to the present times have been presented and livened with the views of critics. An attempt has been made to evaluate the facts as well as the views of critics. Normally, an educational system should be able to preserve the past, enrich the present and provide guidelines for development in the future. So far, the developments are somewhat satisfactory. There are philosophical, social, political, economic and administrative problems which must he tackled, if a system worth its name has to evolve. It is hoped that the policies of the leadership in the Centre and the States will be guided by broad national interests—and not by vote-bank politics.

The authors acknowledge with a sense of humility and a feeling of gratitude, the works, documents and writers consulted and quoted in *Development of Educational System in India.* A book is like the nest, for the making of which, the bird collects straws from everywhere : the nest is, however, a unique structure—perhaps a "system".

Hamirpur
Himachal Pradesh
26 January, 2008

A.S. Thakur
Sandeep Berwal

Introduction

All nations have history : some of them can trace their past, back to thousands of years; some are able to recollect their history of a few hundred years; and some may have just started an introduction to their historical past. India is proud of its glorious past, its stimulating present and its hopeful future. Education dominates the scenes of what was, what is and what will be.

We Indians are proud of our past in that the *Vedas*, the *Upanishads*, the *Gita* are at once profound, sublime, practicable and comprehensive, yet we are not vainglorious to claim that these are written by God Himself. We do acknowledge that our thinkers, seers and writers were inspired beings, but behind the inspirations lay their keen study, wide experience, convincing logic, deep reflection and requisite dynamism. That knowledge is the "third eye" is an aphorism in intellectual humility rather than arrogance.

Education in the Buddha period aimed at *Nirvana* (Salvation). Who would not have aspired for *Nirvana* after he had received education and developed knowledge, character, culture and Buddhism? The universities at Taxila, Nalanda, Vikramshila, Jagdala etc., were renowned centres of higher learning which attracted students from Tibet, Korea and Java. Education was open "for all"—a concept of the present centuries and that too, in some countries only.

During the Middle Ages, 10th to 18th centuries, a new system of education emerged alongwith the Vedic and Buddhist systems : it was the Islamic system of education. In this system, the recitation of the *Quran* was almost compulsory and the new languages—Arabic and Persian—were mastered for spiritual, intellectual and vocational considerations.

The western type of education was brought to India by the Christian missions from the U.K., France, Portugal, Holland etc. The missionaries were so much overwhelmed with the teachings of Christianity that they assumed the non-Christian world to be dark. Spread of the gospel required literacy; thus arose the need for schools. Coastal towns suited their endeavours, although with mixed blessings.

The East India Company, though a trading enterprise, got interested in education as well as propagation of Christianity. The Company understood the worth of the policy of appeasement both of the Muslims and the Hindus—Warren Hastings opened the Calcutta *Madrassa* in 1781; Jonathan Duncan established the *Benaras Sanskrit* College in 1791; and Lord *Wellesley* established Fort William College at Calcutta. However, the credit for "whitewashing" Indians, perhaps went to Charles Grant, whose views influenced the Charter of 1793, which was so weather-beaten that the Charter of 1813 assigned the responsibility of educating the Indians to the Company and the State.

It is interesting to observe that some Indians were keen on getting the western education. It appears that for them *pathashalaṣ, vihars* and mosques were great seats of learning but the western type of schools with arts and sciences taught through the medium of English were, perhaps, considered greater. Thus, there was controversy: should the Indians be educated in Indian languages and subjects or given English education?

Perhaps, to resolve such controversies there appeared Lord *Macaulay* who, in his capacity as the President of the General Committee of Public instruction, in a single sentence in his Minute of 1835 committed the *Himalayan* blunder when he said that "a single shelf of a good European literature was worth the whole native literature of India and Arabia." How could these words come from a Cambridge University scholar, with the knowledge of Greek, Latin, politics, history and law is baffling? *Macaulay*'s *Minute* was a quinine-coated sugar pill: it hurt the pride of the Indians, but the sweetness of the Western type of education spread from a selected few to majority and ultimately to the masses, in spite of the downwards theory of filteration.

Bentinck's Resolution of 1835 accepted *Macaulay*'s Minute and, though the barriers of caste and religion were removed, the policy was to produce through the western education persons who were "Indians in blood and colour but English in tastes, in opinions, in morals and in intellect"—that is, so to say, for the salves to put on the mantle of the masters.

Sir *Charles Wood* was the President of the Board of Control of East India Company. He never visited India, yet his Depatch of 1854 contained some healing power in that it did not condemn education through the media of *Sanskrit* and Arabic. The vernacular languages became partners with English. Another redeeming factor of the Despatch was that it stressed the need for the establishment of universities which were later established in 1857 at Calcutta, Bombay and Madras. However, the Despatch considered education to produce loyal servants and those whose bent of mind was to encourage sending raw material to the industries in the U.K. and buy the products of these industries. Little wonder that until independence, we bought even the British sewing needles! The *Wood*'s Despatch was a "magna charta", if not a Magna Charta, of education for India.

Bentinck's appointment of priest *William Adam* to survey the state of education in Bengal and Bihar was a step in the right direction, but his researched reports were not acceptable to *Macaulay* as these recognised the value of indigenous schools.

It was in 1882 that an Indian Education Commission under the Chairmanship of *Hunter* was appointed. There were 20 members, including 7 Indians in it. Its recommenda-tions related to indigenous education, primary education, model high school, grants-in-aid, and it offered encouragement to private and missionary enterprises. Historians have viewed the recommendations of the *Hunter* Commission as a harbinger of educational awakening.

Lord *Curzon* was appointed Governor-General of India in 1899. He was an arrogant person. The Indians hated him for his stiff-necked attitude which acted as a double-edged sword: it gave birth to militant nationalism in that the otherwise relaxed necks of nationalists like *Tilak, Lajpat Rai, Pal* and many others, became "stiff" against the colonial administration. The significant events during *Curzon*'s regime were the Education Conference of 1901, Indian Universities Commission of 1902, Government Resolution on Education Policy of 1904, Indian Universities Act of 1904 and National Education Movement of 1905. It seems *Curzon* had love-hate relationship with the Indians—he loved the westernized apolitical Indians but he hated the educated, political Indians.

The salient features of the National Education Movement of the first two decades of the twentieth century included pointing out the weakness of the university education, advocating qualitative improvement in education in general, Indianization of education department, establishing of *swadeshi* education institutions, coming into being of National Council of Education and of national universities: Gurukul at Haridwar, Kashi Vidyapeeth, Jamia Milia Islamia, Aligarh (late Delhi) and Vishwabharati at Calcutta. Education was no longer a shield : it had become a sword in the hands of the nationalists.

Gokhale's Bill of 1910 was a visonary's effort to make elementary education free and compulsory throughout the country. It was, however, rejected because the colonial powers did not consider the people of India ready for primary education. Nevertheless, national education institutions continued to grow and *Gokhale*'s vision become a reality in Bombay soon enough in 1918. The colonial government continued the policy of tinkering with education through educational policy of 1913.

The next attempt at establishing a system of education was made by the Calcutta University Commission under the Chairmanship of Dr. *Sadler* in 1917. The Commission made recommendations relating to Calcutta University but by implication these concerned all other universities in India. Furthermore, the Commission's recommendations related to the Muslim education, teacher training, technology, professional and vocational education, modern Indian languages and secondary education. The Commission mooted the idea of the 10+2+3 structure of education which was adopted much later in 1975. Although the Commission went beyond its brief of concentrating on Calcutta University, yet it did not make recommendations on the quantitative and qualitative improvements in the primary education without which the rungs of the educational ladder to second and higher levels of education were bound to remain weak.

The Government of India Act of 1935 introduced provincial autonomy in eleven provinces of British India in 1937. The provinces became responsible for education also. The year 1937 also marked the launching of the *Wardha* Scheme of Education by *Mahatma Gandhi*. The novelty of the Scheme was its philosophy of education which had also drawn the best from the western world. *Gandhiji* made education craft-centered, activity-oriented, mother-tongue mediated and correlated with child's immediate physical and social environment. In spite of the charge of being psychologically unsound and anti-industrialization—fad, fallacy, farce and fraud—*Gandhiji* presented a point of view on education which had sound foundations and its craft-centred approach led to vocationalisation of education.

Before independence in 1947, a document of some significance was the *Sargent* Report of 1944. It dealt with education at the pre-primary, basic, high school and university levels and technical, commercial, adult and teacher education. The report presented a comprehensive scheme of national education, but it placed a 'tame' idea that India required many years to catch up with England.

After independence, the Government appointed University Education Commission, 1948-49 under the Chairmanship of Dr. *Radhakrishnan*. The Commission laid down the aims of education which were philosophical, scientific, sociological, political, moral, cultural, hisotrical and vocational. The recommendations presented an insightful state of affairs in higher education in that the wisdom, knowledge and skills of the past were to guide action in the present and the present was to provide a road map for the future.

The then, Education Minister, *Maulana Abul Kalam Azad*, wanted fresh outlook and new measures to tackle new India's problems. Secondary Education Commission, 1952-53 under the Chairmanship of Dr. *Mudaliar* was appointed to address the issues relating to secondary education. The Report stated the main objectives of education as: development of democratic citizenship, vocational efficiency, personality development and qualities of leadership. Recommendations like the industrial education cell, provision of higher secondary education according to age, ability and aptitude, educational and vocational guidance, improvement in examination system and keeping of cumulative records made some visual impact, but there was hardly any potent programme of action for implementing its recommendations.

Following on the heals of the two post-independence Commissions, a National Education Commission, 1964-66 was appointed under the Chairmanship of Dr. *Kothari*. In letter and spirit, the *Kothari* Commission embodied the functions of both the earlier Commissions as it dealt with education at all the stages and in all aspects. The essence of the Report was to bring about the needed educational revolution and it observed that "the destiny of India is being shaped in her classrooms." The Commission recommended transformation of the educational system, improvement of quality and expansion in programmes. The Report was considered unique but some pointed at its confusing nature and treated it as if it had sounded the death knell of Basic Education.

In spite of ancient *Vedic* education, Buddhist and Islamic contributions, Christian missionary ventures, hide and seek of the British colonial government, reports of committees and commissions, no virile education policy had been forthcoming until 1968 when a resolution on national policy on education was issued. Some important features of the policy were the introduction of 10+2+3 pattern of education, vocationalization of higher secondary education and establishment of National Institute of Education, Planning and Administration, New Delhi. It was, however, in 1986 that the National Policy on Education was adopted.

The most distinct features of the policy document of 1986 were the formation of the national system of education, restructuring of the curriculum, operation blackboard, establishment of *Navodaya* schools and vocationalisation of education. National system of education drew its inspiration from the ideas of democracy, secularism and socialism. The system is based on common core curriculum. Operation black-board implies provision of adequate space, furniture and aids to teaching. *Navodaya* schools are pacesetting schools for rural, but talented students. Vocationlisation was to cover 10 percent of higher secondary students by 1990 and 25 percent by 1995.

National Policy on Education and the Programme of Action have been reviewed by the *Rammurti* Committee in 1990, the *Janardan Reddy* Committee in 1992 and the *Yashpal Committee* in 1993. The first 10 years of schooling are divided into 5 years of primary, 3 year of upper primary and 2 years of high school. The new thrust is to ensure universal access and enrolment, retention at school of children upto 14 years of age and improvement in quality of education. From the Eighth Five Year Plan onwards, the outlay on education will uniformly exceed 6 percent of the national income. The Programme of Action 1992 is to be jointly implemented by the Union, States and Union Territories. Cost effectiveness and accountability are highlighted. It is proposed to establish linkages between education and other related services. The emphasis is laid on the improvement of women and the disadvantaged section of the country through education. The quantity, quality and variety of the teaching force have been improved, but the image requires improvement: teacher has yet to became "a co-worker with God" in perfecting man.

SECTION–I

VEDIC–BUDDHIST-MEDIEVAL PERIODS

(*HERE AND HEREAFTER*)

1

Development of Education in the Vedic Period

The upsurge to trace one's roots comes either when one's present is dull and drab, and the past has something stimulating to offer, or when the past has been deliberately ignored and a need is felt to appreciate its worth. In case of India, the need to appreciate its past is felt for four reasons. The first reason is that the colonial powers had wanted to exhibit the superiority of their cultures and civilizations, including their education. It was natural for them to de-emphasize, ignore and even deny that India had a glorious past. The second reason is that the western history was made to shine to the extent of having a blinding effect on the Indians. The third reason is that many educated Indians were quite comfortable in being Indians in flesh and blood but whitemen in their repertoire. The fourth reason is that India has come from a state of slogan-shouting to face the realities of the present centuries in which tracing the past is not for basking in its glory, real or imagined, not for running away from the present and not for fearing the future, but it is for assessing her achievements and drawbacks with a view to assigning a genuine place of existence for her.

The study of education during the *Vedic* period is to recognize the fact that we have had a *system* of education many centuries ago. By "system" is meant that there are aims of education; there are motivated learners; there are learned teachers; there are vast sources and resources for studying; and there are diverse methods of teaching. Above all, a system is evaluated for its merits and shortcomings by the inbuilt mechanisms in it. Thus, the assessment of the *Vedic* education for many centuries is carried out by examining its aims, the centres of learning, the learners and their teachers and curriculum considerations: these are, by and large, interrelated and interdependent components of a system.

Aims

The aims of *Vedic* education were individual and social, academic and vocational, spiritual and materialistic, and national and international. In short, the aims were comprehensive.

The aims were individual in the sense that the learner assimilated knowledge and put it into practice. All human beings come with instincts. Some of the instincts are healthy but some are such that, if these are not controlled and sublimated, these can lead persons in the wrong directions. The *Vedic* education taught a person to control and sublimate the harmful tendencies. Nature was regarded as a symbol of divinity and the learner worshipped it with a view to attaining salvation. Through self-control, self-respect, love and sympathy, the learner developed his character and personality.

The social aspect of aims was that learner practised cooperation and loved human beings in general. Congresses of scholars were organized for discussion and prominent scholars were given awards. The *Vedic* education devleoped healthy civic sense. The scholars performed their duties towards children, women and elders. They strictly observed the social norms.

The aims were academic in the sense that a good deal of learning was done for obtaining knowledge for the sake of knowledge. Knowledge obtained from teachers for intellectual enrichment and spiritual advancement did not have any utilitarian value. It was for satisfying one's love for knowledge.

The vocational aim was that the different *Vernas* of people were prepared for the needs of their life—priesthood, fighting, trade, service. Students were trained to earn their living. The wordly aspect of education was to train students in art, craft, industrial and medical education for making comfortable their own life and life of the society. The *Vedic* education ultimately aimed at *moksha* (liberation) or self-realisation. The liberation meant to be free from the cycle of birth and death and be one with God. This was the "other-wordly" aspect of education.

Values inculcated by the *Vedic* education were not narrow. The culture was preserved and transmitted within the country and beyond. Knowledge was considered the 'third eye'. Possibly no one could stop the third eye from seeing inwardly as well as seeing beyond one's own national boundaries.

The aims appear to be diverse but there is an inner link because these prepared the individuals who required and acquired knowledge, skills and wisdom to cope with their wordly life, and at the same time, prepared for life beyond the veil.

Institutions of Learning

As today, the home in the *Vedic* time was the first school of the child. The child learnt both by observation and by being taught by the family. He aquired the language and social behaviour from the family. From the family, the child requiring rich education moved to the residential schools where the learner and teacher lived together.

There were two forms of *Vedic* education: (*a*) verbal self-study and (*b*) meditation. *Vedic rishis* encouraged their sons and grandsons to learn hyms by heart. Later on, other children were also admitted as disciples.

The greatest contribution to *Vedic* education was made by the *gurukula* which was the home of the *acharyas* (teachers). In the *gurukula*, every student was to serve his teacher compulsorily. The students fetched water, twings for brushing the teeth and begged alms to feed themselves and the teacher. But begging for alms was not only to collect items for food but also more to induce humility. Such duties were assigned to the student for self-support, support of the teacher and character building; these did not deprive the student of the main task of studying. Gradually, *gurukulas* were extended and more buildings were used for teaching and learning. Not only was there a horizontal extension, but also a vertical one in that *Parishads*, bigger educational institutions, at which several teachers taught different subjects, came into being. The *Parishads* could be equated with a college of present times.

To exchange views on education, *sammelans* were organised. Scholars gathered at a place for discussions asnd competitions. The kings, many of whom were patrons of learning, invited scholars to such exercises. But education in the *Vedic* era was free from control of the State or other authorities including the kings. In fact, the kings ensured that the learned *pandits* studied and imparted knowledge without interference from any source. Furthermore, their courts were seats of learning and they invited learned scholars to settle in villages.

It was a common practice for students to travel far and wide to hold discussions with scholars. Additionally, the long sacrificial sessions presented opportunities for obtaining practical and functional knowledge.

The Learners

The *Vedic rishis* passed on the knowledge of hymns to their sons and grandsons who learnt the hymns by heart. By and by, other students also joined as disciples, and rituals, methods and systems were introduced. The outsiders were also treated as the family members. All learners memorised the hyms and meditated.

It was considered not only essential but also a mark of respect for the learners to sit at the feet of the *guru* to gain various aspects of knowledge but importantly to acquire absolute knowledge.

Learners were expected to treat the *acharya* as God. Furthermore, the learners were expected to do fault-free deeds. Whatever gifts were given were presented with happiness, respect and kindness.

A student before receiving the highest knowledge of the *Brahman* was expected to be calm and composed in his mind, self-denying and patient. After completing his education, he was presented to the learned assembly and the teacher exhorted the student to continue the study of the *Vedas*, perform his duties towards the parents, pay regards to the learned persons, and, thus, become great.

The Teachers

The modern idealists have said that the teacher is a co-worker with God in perfecting man. Such an idea was practised by the *Vedic* teachers centuries ago. The *Vedic* teacher was not god but he certainly was god-like as he was the rich book, the eloquent transmitter of the content of the book, the critical evaluator of how much of the book has been internalised by his students and one who made up deficiencies of his students.

A teacher possessed moral and spiritual values at the highest level. The expectations in the sacred scriptures were that the teacher was to teach his pupils the truth exactly as he knew: teach him all his heart and soul. If a teacher was worthy and knowledgeable, students came to him from all directions. In turn, students also travelled in search of learned scholars.

Teacher's role as a preserver of knowledge was to spread it far and wide through the valuable libraries. Knowledge was also preserved by passing it on to pupils of superior intelligence, who passed it on to their pupils when they were qualified and experienced to become teachers themselves.

Some religious texts outlined the duties and obligations of teachers in the *Vedic* times. *Apastamba Dharma Sutra* says that the student gathers his duties from him. *Manu Smirti* says: The teacher, after performing *Upanayana,* teaches his pupils the rules about bodily purity, rules of conduct in every day life, offering fuel stick and adoring *Samdhya.* According to *Yajnavalkya Smriti, guru* performed *Samskaras* and imparted the *Veda. Vishnu Dharamasastra* designated the father, the mother and the *acharyas* as the three highest *gurus* of person. In the views of *Patanjali,* the teacher is compared with an umbrella, sheltering the student and motivating him to overcome his deficiencies. The *Mahabharata* treated a teacher as a profound scholar and eloquent orator, logician and one who had the ability to understand most difficult books.

What emerges out of the holy books is that a teacher is a perfect person—intellectually, socially, logically, spiritually and morally.

The Curriculum

The curriculum of the *Vedic* times was broad-based, *R.K. Mukherjee* and *H.D. Sankalia* listed many common subjects like:

The *Vedas*
The *Puranas*
The *Brahmanas*
Grammar (*Brahma Vidya*)
Philosophical systems (*Vidya*)
Stories of heroes
Mantras
Logic

Debates and Discussions

In addition to the above, there were more subjects of study—general and specific, religious and secular, academic and vocational. Process of instruction was to listen to what teacher teaches, performing a ceremony before reading the *Vedas* and contemplation of the truth before realizing it. The pupils asked questions and the teachers not only answered these, but also discussed the answer with them. Subjects were clarified with the help of examples. Rote memorization was criticised; emphasis was placed on understanding the meanings. The technique of question-answer was used to develop the student's power of reasoning. People could gain education in art, crafts, agriculture and animal husbandry. Sea trade was also practised.

Women were educated at home in domestic science. According to *A.S. Attekar*, women took part in every ritual with their husbands. Yet, there was no discrimination: educational opportunities were open to them. Many got higher education: they were called *Brahman Vadini* and achieved the status of *Risika*. Some of the learned women were called *Devis*. Women were given vocational education like weaving and spinning. They were given *shastriya* and practical education.

Later Vedic Education

Later *Vedic* education at once continued many of the traditions of *Vedic* education, developed a system to pronounce correctly the words contained in the *Vedas*, outlined every day duties in the form of text and elaborated on the systems of philosophy. The period is called the period of the *Brahminic* education. The *Brahmin* priests carried out the ritual duties of saying prayers, reciting *mantras,* performing and looking after religious work.

Thus, education in the *Brahminic* period aimed at the physical, mental and character development of the learner. The learners came from the three *Vaṛnas—Brahmins, Kshatriyas* and *Vaishyas,* but the *Shudras* were deprived of the right to education. The *Varna* system was transformed into a rigid caste system, which still prevails with a little of relaxation. The education of women was also neglected. Sanskrit was the medium of instruction and communication.

Methods of Teaching

Diverse methods of teaching were used to teach and learn difficult knowledge. Some of the methods are outlined as:

- Self-meditation and study: the *guru* gave moral lessons and guidance to the students to memorise and meditate.
- Question-answer method: The student asked a question and the *guru* answered and discussed.
- Enigmatic method: Riddles and puzzles were usual.
- Aphoristic method: Knowledge was compressed in small aphoristic sentences, the understanding of which required a high degree of intelligence.
- Etymological method: The meaning of the word was explained according to its root.
- Mythical method: Myths and parables were used.
- Analogical method: Things not explainable by reasoning were explained by analogies.
- Dialectical method: Analysis was carried out.
- Synthetic method: Synthesis was undertaken.
- Monologic method: When the speaker went on speaking even when there were no listeners.
- Ad hoc method: Answering questions that came suddenly and demanded an answer.
- Regressive method: Putting many successive questions in which every new question carried the learner behind the answer of the previous one.

The methods were used mostly in teaching the holy books, particularly the *Upnishads.*

Evaluation

It is not an easy task to evaluate the *Vedic* system of education which covers centuries together. Nevertheless, it may be said that the system had merits as well as shortcomings.

Merits

(*i*) The system was well-organised.
(*ii*) It developed the personality of the learner adequately through an effort to ensure all round development.
(*iii*) The educator was democratic in his relations with students—princes and paupers, rich and poor.
(*iv*) The system ensured self-sufficiency.
(*v*) Education was universal and free.
(*vi*) Simple living and high thinking prevailed.
(*vii*) The system of education largely met the needs of those times.
(*viii*) Education in the later *Vedic* period developed different methods of teaching and learning.

Limitations

(*i*) The schools emphasised other worldliness, which is not easy to conceptualise except for assuming the noble deeds in this world.
(*ii*) Although the assumption was that students would memorise the learning, some could simply be learning it by rote memory.
(*iii*) Discipline in the system was very hard, leaving little scope for cultivating self-discipline.
(*iv*) Evaluation was very subjective, carried out by the teacher. Many teachers could be gods or 'gods-like' but a few could also be human beings with prejudices.
(*v*) The system was, by and large, based on the recapitulation of the past and was, thus, not progressive and forward looking.
(*vi*) In the later *Vedic* education, the *Shudras* and women were not given the opportunities for education.

Conclusion

The wisdom of the past was disseminated to the learners without any discrimination for a long period by the *rishis* and *rishi*-like teachers. Some prejudices did surface against the *Shudras* and women in the *Brahminic* system. It may be said that the *Vedic* education in India showed light to the world, the larger parts of which were either 'dim-lit' or 'dark'. When we Indians get disenchanted of the present and feel uncertain of the future, we travel to seek solace in the past: that past remains incomplete without the *Vedic* period.

Points to Remember

1. Study of the past acquaints us with the contributions, strengths and limitations of educational systems to provide guide to action in the present.
2. The aims of *Vedic* education were individual and social so that character of the learner is developed to function effectively in this world and prepare for the other worldliness.
3. The aims were mainly realised at the *gurukulas,* although learners went around in search of teachers and good teachers attracted students.
4. Students resided at the house of the teachers, performed certain chores at his house and, in turn, the *guru* taught and fed students. Later, bigger institutions came into being to meet the needs of students.
5. *Vedic rishis* passed on the knowledge of hymns to their sons and grandsons. Other students also joined as disciples and lived at the house of the teachers—'*gurukulas*'. Later, other scholarly teachers taught students and students sought teachers, although *gurukulas* continued as seats of learning, headed by the *acharya*.
6. The curriculum comprised the *Vedas,* the *Puranas,* the *Brahmans,* philosophical system, *Mantras* and logic etc. Many methods were used to disseminated and master knowledge.
7. The later *Vedic* period, also known as the *Brahaminic* education, aimed at character development, but was not available to *Shudras* and women.

EXERCISES

1. What do you learn from the history of your past educational system?
2. What were the aims of the *Vedic* system of education?
3. Compare the role of learners in the *Vedic* period with that of the learners in the modern times.
4. Examine the role of teacher in the *Vedic* education. Can we have such teachers today?
5. What curriculum meets the requirements of the *Vedic* aims of education?
6. Comment on the statement that the *Vedic* aims of education were limited in scope.
7. How does the knowledge of the *Vedic* system of education influence you as a teacher?

2

Education in the Buddhist Period

It seems that the *Vedic* and later on the *Brahmanic* education covered a period from 5000 B.C. to 200 B.C. It is a long social, cultural and educational period. Many ills had crept into the *Brahmanic* system of education—domination of religion and ritualism, emphasis upon philosophy, deprivation of right to education for the *Shudras* and women and tendency to hamper logical and rational thought were the serious ills. The society felt that life for it was aimless. A kind of socio-religious vacuum was created. To fill the vacuum appeared the Buddha.

Mahatma Buddha and Swami Mahavira were the only two persons who renounced their thrones and worldly life to establish and preach Buddhism and Jainism respectably. They were the harbingers of greatness from the palaces to the ordinary run of people. Jesus Christ and prophet Mohammed were in, and with, the people but they too delivered greatness to people by establishing Christianity and Islam.

The greatness of Lord Buddha lies in benefiting from the *Vedic* traditions so far as these suited his own message and adding to the *Vedic* traditions his own overpowering message of Buddhism. Buddhism outlined aims of education, institutions of learning for realizing the aims, role of pupils and teachers and curriculum. But it is important to have some knowledge of the Buddhist philosophy.

Buddhist Philosophy

The Buddhist philosophy is based on some noteworthy tenets. Some of these tenets are:

(*i*) Four noble truths—(*a*) all existence involves suffering, (*b*) suffering is caused by desire, especially the desire for the continuance of existence, (*c*) the suppression of desire leads to the extinction of suffering, (*d*) the deliverance can be effected by the eight-fold path: right view or belief, right resolve, right speech, right behaviour, right occupation, right effort, right contemplation, and right concentration.

(*ii*) Eight-fold path for attainment of *nirvana.*

(*iii*) Moral code

(*iv*) Middle path

(*v*) Equality

(*vi*) *Ahimsa*

(*vii*) Silence over the existence of God

(*viii*) No belief in rituals

(*ix*) Belief in rebirth and *karma.*

The metaphysics of Buddhist philosophy of education was the primacy of mind in all men's thought and action: path to self-realisation lay through purity of mind. Mind was the forerunner of all mental phenomena. The epistemology was to apply the standards of reason and logic to all philosophies, ideas and practices.

Aims of Buddhist Education

Aims of the Buddhist education were individual and social, academic and vocational, earthly and heavenly. The aims were individual because great care was taken in the formation of character and development of personality. Physical, moral and intellectual aspects were looked after. Through celibacy and simple food, purification of the soul was expected. Sympathy and pity were stressed. Individuals were trained in the monasteries to understand the grief of others.

Aims were social in that students were taught collectively and there was a good deal of interaction among them. They were to be useful to the society.

Aims were academic as learners acquired knowledge and wisdom for the intrinsic value of them. Aims were vocational because curriculum included agriculture, dairy farming, art, craft, handwork, commerce, military training, spinning and weaving for worthwhile living. Aims were heavenly in that Buddhist education was thoroughly informed by the Buddhist culture and ethos. Through religious education one prepared oneself for salvation (*nirvana*). The aims were, thus, comprehensive.

Institutions of Learning

Generally, the Buddhist education was imparted in *maths, vihars* and monasteries. Monasteries were the main centres of learning. When a student desired to enter a monastery for being educated, he approached a teacher and requested him to educate him. The teacher accepted him as his student; he was not accountable to any other teacher (*bhikshu*). At the age of eight, the students started with first ordination ceremony called *pabhaja* which meant going out. The student renounced his family and worldly relationship. He did not belong to any caste after being admitted to a monastery. He got his head shaved fully and put on yellow clothes. He was presented to the head *bhikshu* who advised him thus:

(*i*) I take refuse with Buddha
(*ii*) I take refuse with religion
(*iii*) I take refuse with the order

The student was then called *shraman*.

The ceremony continued for twelve years. After his education for twelve years, the student at twenty underwent the *upasampada* ceremony. In this ceremony, the *shraman* was presented before all other monks of the monastery. He was entitled to the full membership of the monastery and remained a monk for good.

Wherever Buddhist monasteries or *vihars* were established, education centres also emerged. Higher centres of learning, equivalent to universities, developed at Ballabhi, Jagdala, Nadia, Nalanda, Odantpuri, Taxila and Vikramshila. It may be acknowledged that availability of universities demonstrated the democratic feelings of those times.

Of all the universities, Nalanda was the most famous. The Buddhist universities were in the charge of an eminent *bhikshu*, known for his age, learning and character. There were councils for running administrative and academic work. The universities were housed in huge buildings. The corporate character of the institutions ensured high intellectual environment and efficient administration.

The higher level of education in the universities attracted students from as far as Java, Tibet, China and Korea. India of even those times had international reputation.

Education, however, started in the primary schools also. It was materialistic education. Students were six years old and were prepared for leading ordinary life and not like that of the monks.

The Pupils

The student admitted to the *sangha* was to obey the following rules:

- Not to kill any living being: non-violence was expected.
- Not to accept anything given to him: be free from temptations.
- Live free from the impurity of character: pure character was expected.
- Not to tell a lie: follow truth.
- Not to use any intoxicating thing: be a teetotaller.
- Not to take food at improper time: not be a glutton.
- Not to speak ill of any body: be generous.
- Not to take any interest in music, dance, play show, etc: be free from temptations.
- Not to use luxurious and scented things: lead a Spartan life.
- Not to accept the gift of gold or silver etc.: be free from greed.

These commandments set the pattern of life for the students. These were observed by new monks.

However, a student was not admitted until he has been permitted by his parents; he was free from infectious diseases; he was not convicted of any serious moral sin; he was free from legal bondage; and he was found hard working and generous during the period of probation—generally four or five days after being admitted.

Students served their teacher, arranging water, looking after his meal, cleaning the utensils, and going out for alms with him. Students bathed themselves and got ready for education which was imparted following the system of the day. The student obeyed none else but his teacher. He took permission to go out. In short, disciples were under the firm control of their teacher. The disciple gained knowledge while serving his teacher. If the teacher was in some mental trouble, students amused him by religious conversations and other means. The pupil-teacher relationship was informed by affection, confidence and reverence.

The monks and students followed the principle of "simple living and high thinking"—simple living leaves a lot of time for high thinking. To start with, women were not allowed to join the monasteries. They were treated as evils. Later, women were permitted to join the monasteries but there were many restrictions on them like not meeting male monks. It may be said that Buddhism was not favourable to education of women.

The Teachers

The teacher was well read, efficient and of high moral character. He used various methods—lecture, question-answer—to enable his students to gain full knowledge and attain *nirvana*. The teacher was wholly responsible for education, food, clothes and residence of a student monk. The teacher got a sick student treated. He showered all his affections on a student.

The Curriculum

(*a*) **Subjects**: The Buddhist education was mainly meant for attaining *nirvana*: it was, thus, religious like the *Vedic* education. At the primary level, education, based on the *Jatakas* and stories, was for worldly purposes. Children of six years of age joined the primary school and continued until the twelfth year. Instruction was given in reading, writing, arithmetic and religion. As recorded by traveller Hieun Tsang in the 7th century A.D., children were also taught grammar, logic, science of reasoning, inner science, arts and crafts, and medicine. The languages of instruction were Sanskrit and Pali. There was taught *Tripataken*. After the monks mastered these subjects, they were taught works on Buddhist religion and philosophy. The *Vedas* were replaced by Buddhist literature. Those intended to be monks were not taught 'secular' subjects like literature, poetics, astrology etc.

During the Buddhist period, subjects relating to Buddhism were Buddhist literature and knowledge about the monasteries. But the parallel *Brahmanical* education continued teaching the *Vedas*, the *Puranas*, grammar, rhetorics, systems of philosophy, hymns, military science etc.

It was at the university level that education, say at Taxila, related to the *Vedas*, *Vedanta*, grammar, *Ayurveda*, craft, military science, astrology, agriculture, commerce, treatment of snake bite and magical charms. Similar subjects were taught at other universities, with addition or deletion of one or two subjects.

(*b*) **Methods:** A number of methods were used so that a teacher of perfect knowledge could impart it to his pupils to make them perfect.

- *Verbal education*: As there was paucity of written material, teachers gave lessons to the novices asking them to learn these by heart. Also, monks were sent to nearby places to gain oral knowledge of things.
- *Discussions*: Rules were framed for discussion, e.g., discussion was on a useful subject and orgainsed at a place where scholars congregated or at the royal palace or minister's office and assembly. Discussion was also used as a tool against critics.
- *Evidence*: It was like the modern debate. The person was expected to be well versed in the subject and eloquent in presentation. The arguments were supported by logic.
- *Tours:* The monks were sent on tours to observe things and experience events. The knowledge thus gained could be passed on to others.
- *Conferences:* Conferences were held in the *sanghs*. Here, the monks discussed their doubts and decided punishment for those who might have shown moral laxity.

At an annual conference, a renowned monk challenged the moral purity of the entire *sangh* and the challenge was defended.

- *Mediation in solitude*: Some monks after learning in the *sangh* retired to the calm of forests and caves to meditate. Similarly, old monks who had discharged their obligations in the *sanghs* retired to the forest and caves for meditation.
- *Assembly of learned monks*: Once a year, scholarly monks assembled to hear the cases of monks who had confessed their immoral behaviour. After deliberation, punishment was awarded. Sometimes an accused monk, if innocent, defended himself. Such democratic interaction was to ensure high moral standards.
- *Mass education*: When monks went out to beg for alms, they talked to the people and answered their questions and removed their doubts. Spiritual and moral discourse and advice had a positive impact on the behaviour of common people.

Learning within the *sanghs* and monasteries, discussions, confession, travel, interactions and contemplation all contributed to the development and dissemination of the Buddhist education.

Evaluation

Evaluation of Buddhist education, like other systems of education, is concerned with contributions and limitations.

Contributions of Buddhist Education

(*i*) Buddhist education aimed at moral, intellectual and religious development and through various means and methods, it succeeded in realizing the aims.

(*ii*) The main objective was salvation, but preparation was also made for worldly life through vocational education.

(*iii*) Simple living and high thinking protected students from indulging in sensuous pleasures, leaving time for high intellectual and deep spiritual pursuits.

(*iv*) Teacher was held in high esteem not because he desired it but because he deserved it by virtue of his intellectual capability, moral standing, professional zeal and humane nature.

(*v*) Students were admitted irrespective of castes and they were not discriminated against on any ground.

(*vi*) The curriculum was rich, particularly at the university level. Diverse methods were used to teach.

(*vii*) Teachers gave their best to the students, but students also learnt through independent thinking, self-study and meditation.

(*viii*) Buddhist education benefited from the *Vedic* and *Brahmanic* streams of education and made its original contribution also.

Limitations of Buddhist Education

(*i*) Scriptures as an absolute authority discouraged independent thinking and reasoning. The result was a setback to originality.

(*ii*) Buddhism could not eliminate the caste discrimination. The result was that much of the general public remained illiterate.

(*iii*) Dominance of religious concerns inhibited the development of material prosperity.

(*iv*) Slowly, arbitrariness developed, corruption became rampant and there was social decay.

(*v*) Too much emphasis on non-violence did not permit the development of military infrastructure. Thus, military organization was weak.

(*vi*) Education of woman was an exception rather than a rule.

Conclusion

Buddhist education made a good start at a time when the *Brahmanical* education was full of prejudices and other ills. It spread the reputation of India beyond its borders as students came from Java, China and Tibet etc., to get knowledge at its universities. Its curriculum was so rich that students could get religious as well as secular education—education for this world and for the other worldliness. The *Vedic* and the Buddhist systems of education were nearly immortal systems and the incoming Islamic and western systems could not bring these two systems to an end.

Points to Remember

1. The Buddhist period of education carried forward some of the practices of the *Vedic* and *Brahmanic* times, but it made its own contributions also.
2. Buddhist philosophy is based on four noble truths—all existence involves suffering; suffering is caused by desire; suppression of desire leads to its extinction; and deliverance.
3. Aims of Buddhist education were individual and social, academic and vocational, and earthly and heavenly.
4. The aims were realised in the *vihars* and monasteries, primary and secondary schools, and universities.
5. The learners were mostly monks, initially all male, but later some women were also admitted to the monasteries with a lot of restrictions.
6. Teachers were monks who were well read, of high moral character and kind and fair.
7. The curriculum was restricted to the three R's and religion at the primary but broad at the secondary level and was rich at the university level.
8. Buddhist education was democratic and had international appeal.
9. Buddhist education later degenerated because of arbitrariness and corruption.
10. The education continued in the Muslim and western periods of education.

EXERCISES

1. Examine the aims of the Buddhist education for their effectiveness in the Buddhist period.
2. What were the various centres of learning in the Buddhist period? Were these equally famous?
3. How did the students pass through various stages of their school life?
4. What were the roles of the teachers?
5. Elaborate on the following statement: "From a narrow base, the Buddhist education acquired a broad top"—Authors.
6. What are the strengths and weaknesses of the Buddhist education?

3

Education During the Mediaeval Period

Mediaeval period in the history of Europe refers to the period between A.D. 1100 and 1400. But the medieval period in terms of education in India starts from about A.D. 1000 and continues until the middle of A.D. 1800. During this period, three system of education are discernible—The Hindu system managed to survive as a result of the scholars and wealthy people and the Buddhist education continued through its inbuilt system of rationality. Muslim education was conpicuous by its State support.

Muslim Education: Historical Background

Prophet Mohammad attached a great importance to education: he said that "of all the gifts that parents can give to their children, the best is the gift of a liberal education. The ink in the pens of students is purer and nobler than even the blood of martyrs".

When the Muslims rulers invaded India and later settled there, they established educational institutions. Additionally, the Indian culture came under the influence of the Arab culture which had largely come under the influence of Islam. Islam directed the social life of the kings. Muslim ruler like *Muhammad Gori* constructed mosques and schools in Ajmer; his successor, *Kutubuddin,* continued the tradition and later rulers also built mosques, *maktabs* and *madrasas.*

When the *Tuglak* dynasty came into power, it also established schools. For example, *Ferozshah Tuglak* established a huge school in Delhi. Institutions were given grants by the government and scholarships were awarded to students.

It is interesting to note that during the reign of *Sikandar Lodhi* (1489-1519), the Hindus had started learning Persian with a view to taking up administrative jobs under the rulers. Gradually, a new language, Urdu, evolved by the mixture of Hindi and Persian.

Among the Mughal rulers, *Akbar's* name stands out for getting translated into Persian the *Ramayana*, the *Mahabharata*, the *Atharvaveda* and *Lilawati*. *Jahangir* enacted a law to use the proceeds of the property of a dead person without heir for repairing schools and religious buildings. *Shahjahan* was famous as well as notorious—famous for building a university at Aurangabad and notorious for propagating Islamic education. *Aurangzeb*, though a scholar himself, had a blind spot for the Hindu schools.

After the fall of the Mughal empire, schools suffered for lack of organization and finances. Nevertheless, the Hindu system of education continued in *pathashalas, maths* and *temples.* Perhaps it was because of the onslaught of some Muslim rulers on the Hindu system of education and emaciated Muslim education that made the French traveller, *Bernier*, describe the period as of "universal ignorance."

Objectives of Muslim Education

The objectives of various Muslim rulers were somewhat different e.g., of benign *Akbar* and cruel *Aurangzeb*—however, some common aims are as stated below:

Religious Aims

The main focus of the Muslim rulers was on propagating Islam. This was done by means of establishing mosques and attaching *maktabs* to them. The knowledge of *Quran* was imparted in the *maktabs*. Secondly, the major laws of Islam and the *shariyats* of the *Quran* were taught and these determined the moral criteria for the Muslims to follow. Rules of conduct were rigorously observed. Students were also prepared for attaining salvation.

Vocational Aims

The Islamic education made provisions for vocational, technical and professional education. *Ain-i-Akbari* states that every boy ought to read books on morals, arithmetic, the notation, peculiar to arithmetic, agriculture, mensuration, geometry, astronomy, physiognomy, household matters, the rules of government, medicine, logic the *tabi'i, riazi,* and *ilahi* sciences, and history. Professor *Weber's* appreciation of delicate woven fabrics, masterpieces in metal and precious stones, and magnificent buildings is the result of vocational education imparted during the medieval period. The posts of *kazis* and *wazirs* required good education.

Cultural Aims

The Islamic system of education took pains to preserve and transmit culture. Persian and Arabic were used as media of instruction. Original works were studied. There were many international centres of learning in the country—Agra, Delhi, Bihar, Jaunpur being the famous ones.

Political Aims

The Muslim rulers were aware of the situation in which they required the expertise of people, Muslim or non Muslim—obtained through education to run their administration. In fact, many Hindus also rose to high positions in the system.

Individual Aims

Although all aims affect the individual in various aspects of his development, certain systems emphasise individual aims over other aims. Islamic education aimed at the formation of character through rigorous discipline and by subjecting students to lead simple and pious life.

The Learners

The child in new clothes was taken to the *maktab*. As the Islamic education was predominantly religious, the child was asked to repeat a few verses from the *Quran*. In case, the child was unable to do so, the word *bismillah* was pronounced. It meant that the child had begun in the name of *Allah* (God). After the *bismillah* ceremony, the child wrote something for a few days and his close relatives were invited to see him. The child was expected to come to the *maktab* regularly. After completing education in the *maktab*, he was sent to *madarasa* for higher education.

Discipline was strictly enforced and teachers were empowered to give different types of physical punishment—caning, slapping, whipping etc., were common in case of delinquent behaviour. There was, thus, some decline in pupil-teacher relationship in contrast with the *Vedic* times. Nevertheless, pupils were expected to serve the teacher, for they sometimes got free food, but always got free knowledge from him. Monitorial system was in vogue, and bright students were rewarded.

The girl students were educated along with the boys up to a certain level. As the girls grew up, they received education at home. Such restrictions had an inhibiting effect on girl's education. The princesses were taught Arabic, Persian and Islamic knowledge.

The Teachers

The teachers were learned scholars. They took to teaching for spreading knowledge and turning out pupils who were useful to themselves and the society, and were also trained for the 'hereafter'. They did not receive high salaries, but they commanded respect of their students and in some cases of the society. They were strict disciplinarians and did not hesitate to punish the wrong-doers. On the other hand, they used monitors to assist them in teaching and rewarded the bright and disciplined students. As there was examination system, it was the teacher who promoted pupils to proceed to the higher class. Perhaps, teachers were fair in their evaluation. *Maulavis* taught children of the royal families in the palaces under strict control and discipline. They gave theoretical as well as practical education.

Institutions of Learning

Islamic education started in the *maktab*, which can he equated with a primary school. Generally, like the *upnayana* ceremony of the *Vedic* period and the *pabbaja* ritual of the Buddhist period, education of the child started with the ritual of *bismillah* at the age of 4 years, 4 months and 4 days. At the *maktab*, the teacher (*maulavi*) taught writing from the *Quran*, *namaz* (prayers), *azzan* (call for prayers), arithmetic, letter writing, conversation, drafting etc. When the child was well acquainted with Persian, he was introduced to love literature like *Laila-Majnu*, *Yusuf-Julekha* etc. Hindu boys were also admitted to the *maktabs*.

After completing education in the *maktab*, one entered *madarasa* for higher education. The kings granted *Jagirs* (land and villages) for the maintenances of *madarasas*. Financial grants were also given by kings and rich people gave financial assistance. But the kings did not interfere in the administration of the *madarasa*. The *madarasa* was headed by a learned scholar and he was assisted by other teachers. Some *madarasas* had hostel accommodation, provided recreational facility like a swimming pool and medical care like a hospital.

The Curriculum

The *maktab* introduced learners to the *Quran*. Teacher dictated and learners wrote on the *takhtis* (wooden slate). Learning of Arabic and Persian was almost compulsory. Stress was on calligraphy. Grammar was taught as it was considered important to the mastering of languages. *Paharas* (multiple of numbers) were memorized loudly. Other than the *Quran*, poems like *Gulistan* and *Bostan* by *Firdausi*, *Karim* by scholar *Sadi* and *Pandnama* by *Attar* were studied.

In the *madarasa*, the *Quran*, Islamic law, sufism, literature, logic, history, geography, astronomy, arithmetic, astrology, agriculture and medicine were taught. Later, *Akbar* added more secular subjects for students.

In terms of methods of teaching, memorizing a book was common. Discussions and seminars were also held for better comprehension; examinations were both oral and written, assessed by teachers concerned.

Evaluation

To evaluate education of the middle ages is not easy as there were two other tributaries—the *Vedic* and the Buddhist—and the main stream, Islamic education. Here, it is the Islamic education that is evaluated, both for its strengths and weaknesses.

Strengths

(*i*) Education was compulsory, particularly for boys.

(*ii*) There was coordination between the aims—individual and social, material and spiritual, academic and vocational.

(*iii*) Character formation was emphasized by exemplary life of the teachers and by preaching about noble life.

(*iv*) Relationship between the teacher and taught was intimate as the focus was on individualized instruction and close supervision of the learner by the teacher. Meritorious students were rewarded.

(*v*) The curriculum was wide ranging: focus was on religious knowledge but subjects of academic and vocational significance were also included. Literature developed and studying and writing of history helped in procuring records.

(*vi*) Starting with *maktabs* and ending with *madarasas* produced the semblance of a structure of schooling, if not a system.

(*vii*) Though dominated by the Muslim learners, the Hindu learners were free to benefit from Islamic education and many Hindu students excelled the Muslim students and rose to high administrative posts.

Weaknesses

(*i*) As students spent a good deal of their time in mastering Arabic and Persian, local languages lagged behind in their development.

(*ii*) Oral method of teaching had its limitations in that there was a limit to how much a learner could hear, understand, retain and recapitulate.

(*iii*) The emphasis on memorization had an adverse effect on the development of the power of reasoning of the learners.

(*iv*) There was no restriction on women education, but the *purdah* system put limitations to the education of the women.

(*v*) The severe corporal punishment was not psychologically justifiable.

Conclusion

Three streams of education—the *Vedic,* the Buddhist, the Islamic—during the middle ages saved the times from the epithet of "dark ages" as it was the case in the European history. The three cultural streams continued until these were later overwhelmed by the British concepts and practices of education and culture.

Points to Remember

1. Middle ages in the history of India start from A.D. 1000 and end till the middle of A.D. 1800.
2. Although the *Vedic* and Buddhist education continued, the centuries were dominated by Islamic education.
3. Prophet *Mohammad* attached a great importance to education.
4. Muslim rulers constructed mosques and established schools.
5. The aims of Islamic education were religious, but later on academic, vocational, cultural and social considerations also acquired importance.
6. Primary education was imparted in the *maktabs* and secondary or higher education in the *madarasas.*
7. Pupils were mainly boys and started education quite early in their life.
8. Teachers were *maulavis.* Some were not highly regarded by the society, but all were scholarly and devoted to their profession.
9. The curriculum was initially religion-dominated but later academic and vocational subjects were also included. Arabic and Persian were the media of instruction.
10. The Islamic education emphasized character formation and vocational success.
11. The Islamic education, somewhat, lacked in psychological foundations.

EXERCISES

1. Examine the historical background to Islamic education in India.
2. What were the aims of Islamic education?
3. Was the structure of schooling in Islamic education adequate?
4. Comment on the curriculum of Islamic education.
5. What are the merits of Islamic education?
6. Assess the limitations of Islamic education.
7. How does a modern teacher benefit from the knowledge of Islamic education in the middle ages?

SECTION–II

COLONIAL PERIOD
(*HIDE AND SEEK*)

4

Western Education: Macaulay's Minute, Bentinck's Resolution and Adam's Reports

In the previous chapters, we strode along centuries of history of the *Vedic* times, the Buddhist apoch and the middle age to reach the nineteenth century. In this chapter, we have tried to trace the steps which enable us to see as well as visualise the development of western type of education in India. To call it a system will be a misnomer, as somewhat of a system worth its name developed much later from 1986 onwards.

Christian Missions

A semblance of western education was brought to India by the Christian missions. They spread their proselytizing and educational work in the coastal areas. Among the missions, the Roman Catholic, the Anglican, the Franciscan, the Dominican and the Jesuit started their work in the eastern, southern and western coastal towns. St. Xavier and St. Loyala in the south, the Dutch in Bengal, the French at Mahe and Pondichery and the Dane at Tanjore and Srirampur undertook educational and conversion work. The European missionaries were convinced, perhaps naivaly, that Asia and Africa—Africa in particular—were "dark continents", and to show them light was the holy task. Education became a necessity as their congregations had to read the Bible, later translated into the Indian vernaculars. The four Rs—reading, writing, arithmetic and religion—dominated the scene. The missions continued their activities—even increased them.

The East India Company

The East India Company, established in 1599 for trading with India, became financially so strong that it also made spread of Christian religion its goal. The Company first adopted a policy of religious indifference that was to stop financial aid to schools. But later in 1771, *Warren Hastings* opened the Calcutta *madarasa;* in 1781, *Jonathan Duncan* established the Banaras Sanskrit College; and in 1800 Lord *Wellesley* established Fort William College at Calcutta.

Initial British Concern

The beginning of the British concern with education of the Indians could to traced back to Charles Grant who in 1772 proposed:

(*i*) The establishment of schools in India.
(*ii*) Education through English medium.
(*iii*) Free education for English language and literature.
(*iv*) Expansion for western science and knowledge.
(*v*) Wide publicity for Christianity.

Influenced by the view of *Grant*, *William Wilberforce* proposed to raise the level of knowledge, religion and morality of the Indians in the Charter of 1793. Grant's proposal was rejected. The remark by *Nurullah* and *Naik* that *Grant* was the father of modern education in India is not tenable because his proposals were not accepted, he stood for free education for English language and literature, showing his insular thinking, and he seems to have become a priest in championing the cause of Christianity. Moreover, he treated the Hindus as ignorant, forgetting their continuity with the rich *Vedic* tradition in education.

Next came the Charter of 1813 in which the Company was again asked to educate the Indians but the proposal had no effect. On the other hand, Lord *Minto* made arrangements for providing a sum of ten thousand pounds per year for education. This may be taken to be the beginning of the system of grant-in-aid of education.

In the year 1831 was established a General Committee on Public Instruction, which emphasized the utilitarian aspect of knowledge. The Committee faced the problem of objectives, media and means of education and, thus, expressed views along three lines—one group wanted education imparted through Sanskrit, Arabic and Persian, the second group advocated English as the medium of instruction, and third view stood for regional languages. All these three views were held by the employees of the Company.

But more people—British and Indian—joined the debate between orientalists and the occidentialists. Education secretary in Bengal, *H.T. Princep*, joined the orientalists; *Raja Ram Mohan Roy* supported the occidentialists: the former supported Indian languages and the latter supported English as the medium of instruction.

It was in 1834 that Lord *Macaulay* was sent as the Law Member of the Company. Lord *Bentick* also made him the Chief of the Public Instruction Committee. *T.H. Macaulay* was well educated man; he was a writer of repute and he was a remarkable parliamentarian, backed by his law studies and oratorical skills. One would have expected of him intellectual discipline, social acumen, broadmindedness and reverence for other religions. But, he, in his Minute of 1835, betrayed the presence of these characteristics.

Macaulay's Minute

Macaulay wrote his famous (or notorious) minute and submitted it to the Executive Council of Governor General on 2nd February, 1835. Some of the noteworthy views on India, the Indians and the Indian culture and civilization were:

- A single shelf of a good European library was worth the whole native literature of India and Arabia.
- English language was the most florishing and useful of all European languages.
- Vast treasure of knowledge had been created by the most intelligent race of the world.
- The higher classes living in the capitals in India spoke English.
- English may become the language of the trade on Eastern seas.

- Educate the higher classes and they could teach the lower classes—theory of downward filtration.
- The higher classes should be Indians by colour and blood, but English by interest, morality and intellect.
- The British Parliament in 1813 had set the sum of money, not for the promotion of literature of Sanskrit and Arabic, but for the promotion of learning which would enable the natives to be familiar with the poetry of Milton and the physics of Newton. Money should no longer be employed in encouraging Arabic and Sanskrit.
- We are to teach false history, false astronomy, false medicine, because we find them in company of a false religion. In India there was absurd physics, absurd metaphysics, absurd theology.
- We are a Board for wasting public money for printing books which are of less than value of the paper on which they are printed while it was blank.
- If, on the other hand, it be the opinion of Government that the present system ought to remain unchanged, I beg that I may be permitted to retire from the Chair of the Committee.

Macaulay's Minute: Facts and Fiction

- Macaulay did not know Sanskrit, Arabic or Persian. For him to boast of a "shelf" of a good European library being of more worth than the whole literature of India and Arabic was a historical lie. Literature in Sanskrit, Arabic and Persian was old, rich and diverse. When the *Vedas* were available, the Europeans, including Englishmen, were, perhaps cave dwellers?
- English language which he claimed to be the most flourishing and useful of all European languages was not correct—at least German and French were comparable with English, if not superior to it.
- To claim British 'race' to be the most intelligent one was simply blowing one's own trumpet. In fact, the Germans and the French would be more annoyed at this statement than Indians.

- In saying that the higher classes in capitals spoke English in India, *Macaulay* was transporting the class hierarchy of England to India. There were no classes as such in India at that time.
- English had already become language of trade in Eastern seas through the work of the Christian missions.
- The theory of downward filtration was educationally unsound: education is a pyramidal venture with a broad base and not so narrow top.
- The attempt to brainwash Indians to be like the English in their repertoire succeeded to some extent, but the contemptuous term *'babu'* was—and—is used for Indians who tend to be like the English.
- *Macualay* took full advantage of the decision of the British Parliament in 1813 to allot a sum of money for the promotion of literature. Obviously Indian literature, as there was no other literature—so to say, by overwriting that the money was for the study of *Milton's* poetry and *Newton's* physics, he betrayed his prejudice against Sanskrit, Arabic and Persian.
- In fact, it was *Macaulay* who tried to write false history as Indian history might have been sketchy, but it was true. Indian astronomy was the work, not only of instruments, but also of human intellect, observations and conclusions. Systems of Indian medicine were based on experience and research. *Macaulay* failed to understand that when he wrote his Minute, Christianity was about 1800 years old, whereas Hinduism was over 5000 years old. Moreover, it was sacrilegious on his part to look down upon other religions. It seems that there was a blank wave in a part of his brain which prevented him from recognizing that no religion is false: religion is the voice of God—heard, understood, recognized and propogated by prophets, devotees, saints and *yogis* in different periods of history. The Hindu *rishis* heard the voice of God thousands of years ago, *Jesus* heard it and *anno domino* started and prophet *Mohammad* heard it between 570 A.D. and 632 A.D.

- Books are printed so that these are read to gain knowledge. These are not mainly for earning profit. *Macaulay's* observations that books printed in Sanskrit, Arabic and Persian bring no profit betrayed the thinking of a petty trader.
- *Macaulay's* veiled threat to resign from the Chair of the Committee was an attempt to blackmail Lord *William Bentinck*. *Macaulay* succeeded largely, though not totally, in seeing through his views.
- It may be said that in spite of his rhetoric and invectives, *Macaulay* was the pioneer of western type of education in India. The urge was already there as expressed by Raja *Rammohun Roy*. Some Indians saw the economic advantages of western education. Ultimately, some western educated Indians exhibited their nationalistic sentiment and demanded freedom for India.

Bentinck's Resolution, 1853

Bentinck in a single line, "I give my entire concurrence to the sentiments expressed in this minute" accepted *Macaulay's* view and embodied them in the resolution. A summary of the resolution is that:

- European literature and science be promoted among the natives of India.
- Funds be best employed on English education alone.
- Colleges or schools of oriental learning should continue.
- Funds were not to be spent in printing oriental books.
- Funds saved were to be used in imparting knowledge of English literature and science through the medium of English.

S.N. Mukherjee's remark that 'the British policy brought about the dawn of a cultural renaissance after centuries of confusion and darkness' is unacceptable. First, it was not at all cultural renaissance but cultural aggression. British culture was imposed on the so-called higher classes. There were no dark ages: the *Vedic,* the Buddhist and the Islamic education had shown the light which might have flickered but had never failed.

It may, however, be said that *Bentinck's* declaration tried to put an end to the oriental-occidental controversy. But after his resignation and departure for England, *Metcalf* took over and the controversy still continued. After *Metcalf*, Lord *Auckland* became the Governor-General. He decided to give financial assistance to both the groups.

Downward Filtration Policy of Education

In 1830, the Directors of the East India Company had written to Madras Government that :

> "the improvements in education, however, which most effectually contribute to elevate the moral and intellectual condition of a people are those, which concern the education of the higher classes of the persons possessing leisure and natural influence over minds of their countrymen. By raising the standard of education among these classes you will eventually produce a much greater and more beneficial change in the ideas and feeling of the country than you can hope to produce by acting directly on the numerous class."

Macaulay in 1835 and 1837 produced similar ideas. The reason could be that the minds of the British rulers were conditioned by the class structure of their own society: high, middle, low—university education for the higher, secondary education for the middle and elementary education for the lower classes. So all people in the Company or the Government seem to have thought alike. But more pragmatic reason was that the British Government required Indian manpower of different levels of education—a few for managing the top echelons, more for middle level and still more for the lower levels. The theory did not work in terms of human relations. The lower level masses, though deferential to the yellow *sahibs*, were contemptuous of their high standing, western style, prosperity and rapport with the British—the brown *sahibs*. A cleavage was created between the higher classes and the masses. It may also be said that the downward filtration process was likely to pass on the dregs to the masses—if at all the process would have worked.

Adam's Reports on Education

William *Adam,* a Christian priest of Buddhist faith, came to India in 1818 and spent nearly three decades. He was impressed by the view of India that there was one almighty God. He was closely associated with *Raja Ram Mohan Roy*: both sides were mutually influenced. Lord *Bentinck* appointed him to survey the state of education in Bengal and Bihar and suggest reforms. He submitted three reports between 1835-1838.

First Report

The report contained educational data. *Adam* reported that school existed for every 400 persons in every village—altogether about 100,000 schools. By schools he meant places in which instructions in the element of knowledge were communicated and which had been originated–and were supported–by the natives themselves in contradiction from those that were supported by religious or by philanthropic societies.

Second Report

In his second report, he investigated Naltore Thana in Rajshahi District. Following were his main findings:

Age of schooling—8-14 years on the average.
Type of schools:

(*a*) Regular schools—27, with 262 students
(*b*) Domestic schools—2360 students.
(*c*) Schools for teaching the *Quran*—11.
(*d*) Elementary schools—10 Bengali and 4 Persian.
(*e*) Sanskrit colleges—38 with 397 scholars.
(*f*) Muslim colleges—Nil.
(*g*) Average number of students in a school—10.
(*h*) Average pay of teachers—Rs. 5-8 per month.
(*i*) Literacy rate—6.1 percent, but 3.1 percent to male and
(*j*) 3.0 female to population.
(*k*) Number of instructed adults— 6, 121.

Third Report

Adam's third report was compiled on the basic data, he collected himself and those collected by his agents. He encountered two difficulties relating to means of travel and communication and suspicions among people as to the motive of the survey. His report was divided into two parts. The first part contained data collected from five districts and the second part contained his proposals for the reform of education in general and indigenous education in particular.

In all the five districts, he found, 1,099 Bengali, 376 Hindi, 353 Sanskrit, 694 Persian, 3 formal Arabic, 28 Arabic, 8 English and 6 girls schools, making a total of 2,567 institutions. Scholars at schools numbered as shown below:

Bengali and Hindi	:	24,250
Sanskrit	:	2,555
Persian and Arabic	:	3,654
English	:	242
Girls	:	214
Total	:	30,915

(The centres of domestic instruction were not included in the above figures.)

The second part of the third report contained proposals for reforming the system. Some of the main proposals were:

(*i*) New textbooks (*i-iv*) in Bengali, Hindi and Urdu were to be prepared by Indians and Europeans.

(*ii*) An examiner was to be appointed for each district for surveying the area, supplying and explaining textbooks to the teachers, and examining teachers on the content of textbooks, distributing grants and supervising teachers' work.

(*iii*) Inspectors were to be appointed to supervise the work of examiners.

(*iv*) The vernacular departments of English schools were to be converted into normal schools for training of teachers.

(*v*) Small grants of land were to be awarded to village schools for their maintenance.

(*vi*) Experimental farms were to be organised for agricultural education.

Adam's Reports: An Evaluation

Adam's proposals were attacked by *Macaulay* and he wrote his scathing criticism to *Auckland* who rejected the proposals. *Adam* resigned in disgust.

There are two schools of thought on the merits or otherwise of *Adam's* Reports. Those conditioned to superior class thinking like *Macaulay, Bentinck, Auckland* and later *Hartog* on the one hand and those who examined the proposals objectively like Commissioner *Adam* himself and later *Parulekar* and others on the other hand. The class conscious category dismissed the Reports as "impracticable and legends".

In defense of the proposals, *Parulekar* found the reports correct. *F.W. Thomas* praised the reports thus: "from the accuracy of its information, the candour, sense and statesmanship of its author (*Adam*), it is among the most valuable and interesting publication on education in India". In a similar vein, *S.N. Mukherjee* assessed *Adam's* Reports as one of the ablest reports ever written on Indian education...a golden opportunity for building up a national system of education, based on culture and languages of the people was lost."

Those who ridiculed and later got rejected *Adam's* Report, forgot that England itself had struggled to promote the vernacular language, English—as against classical Greek and Latin. None other than those behind rejection could have appreciated the important role of supervision and inspection, acquainted as they were with the role of His/Her Majesty's Inspectors. They forgot that the translation of the Bible into English greatly satisfied the urges of the congregation. That each child has an inalienable right to speaking, reading and writing his mother-tongue was known to them, but they were blinded by the glitter of—although not so glittering—English language. That teacher training was as important as training for law and medicine did not cross their minds, perhaps, hypnotized as they were by the idea that "mental discipline" acquired from Cambridge and Oxford degrees could enable people to undertake any task.

Conclusion

The *Vedic,* the Buddhist and the Islamic systems of education continued, but their presence was somewhat eclipsed by the western type of schools, which received British Government's blessings. Perhaps, attitude of 'hide and seek' of the Indians and 'wait and see' of the Christian missions suited the colonial power.

Points to Remember

1. Western education in its rudimentary forms was started by the Christian missions in the coastal areas.
2. The East India Company remained indifferent to the education of the Indians.
3. The British concern with education of the Indians started with *Charles Grant* who in 1772 proposed the establishment of schools. The proposal was not accepted.
4. In 1831 was established a General Committee on Public Instruction.
5. *Macaulay* wrote his Minute in 1935, criticizing Sanskrit, Arabic and Persian and advocating for English education for the higher class and through them education was to filter down to the masses. His views were accepted by Governor-General *Bentinck. Macaulay* has been criticized for his prejudiced views.
6. *Adam,* a Christian missionary, was appointed as a Commissioner by *Bentinck* to report on education in Bengal and Bihar.
7. *Adam* presented three reports. He stood for education through the medium of local languages and made proposals for supervision and inspection of schools. His proposals were rejected and he resigned in disgust.

EXERCISES

1. Examine the role of the Christian missions in the education of the Indians.
2. Why was the East India Company reluctant to providing education to the Indians?
3. Evaluate the educational significance of *Macaulay's* Minute of 1835.
4. Discuss *Grant's* reports as important documents on education in India.
5. What are the merits and demerits of the downward filteration policy on education?

5

The Wood's Despatch, 1854

The Charters of the East India Company were reviewed and renewed after every 20 years. Thus, in 1763, it was *Grant* who wanted to add articles relating to education in India. In 1813, a sum of rupees one lakh was budgeted for the development of education. In 1833, the amount was increased to rupees one million. When the time came for the order of 1833, it occurred to the Directors of the Company to lay down a policy of education. The British Government appointed a Parliamentary Committee comprising people like *Traivelian, Wilson, Dutt* etc. The Committee had, by and large, a complete idea of educational situation in India. The Committee highlighted the position that the development of education in India would not be, in any case, harmful to British Empire and the nature of development had to be taken up urgently The Board of Directors favourably considered the views of the Committee.

On the recommendations of the Committee, the Directors of the East India Company sent a Despatch in 1854, authored by Sir *Charles Wood*, the president of the Board of Control of the Company. As, so to say, had been conventional, the Despatch is called the Wood's Despatch.

The Despatch: Essence and Declaration

The Despatch carried forward the thinking already done by *Grant, Macaulay* and *Bentinck*, though in pungent remarks, it observed:

"The system of science and philosophy which forms the learning of the East abounds with grave errors, and Eastern literature is at best very deficient as regards all modern discovery and improvement."

Declaration in the Despatch

The declaration in the Despatch was quite clear of its intentions when it said that:

"We must empathically declare that the education which we would desire to see extended in India is that which has for its object the diffusion of the improved arts, science, philosophy and literature of Europe, in short, of European knowledge."

Educational Objectives

The following objectives were kept in view in the Despatch.

(*i*) To confer upon the natives of India those vast and material blessings which flow from the general diffusion of western knowledge;

(*ii*) Not only to produce a high degree of intellectual fitness but also to raise the moral character of those who partake of the above advantages;

(*iii*) To supply the East India Company with reliable and capable public servants; and

(*iv*) To secure for England a large and more certain supply of many articles, necessary for manufactures and extensively considered by her population as well as an almost exhaustible demand for the produce of British labour.

An Analysis of the Objetives

The objective (*i*) is arrogantly stated, although western knowledge had certain advantages. In relation to objective (*ii*), it can be stated that the intellectual fitness and moral character of the Indians were in no way inferior to that of the Birtish. In objective (*iii*), "reliability' was considered on a priority basis compared to 'capability' which was more relevant. Stated last, but being the most harmful, is objective (*iv*)—to drain India of her raw material for the British industries and create in India a market for the finished British goods.

Other Recommendations

Wood's Despatch had 100 clauses and it covered various aspects of education. Moreover, the Despatch was based on the study of documents as Wood had not visited India. Thus, it had the advantages as well as disadvantages pertaining to lack of personal knowledge vis-a-vis the documentary evidence.

Indigenous Education

Macaulay was against indigenous education. *Wood*, however, said that, admitting however, the comparative inferiority of indigenous institutions, "we consider that efforts should now be made to encourage them. They have survived severe competition and have thus proved that they possess both vitality and popularity. Indigenous schools deserved encouragement and incorporation in the official system of education."

Primary Education

For primary education, the Despatch said that:

> "the elementary education of the masses, its provision, extension and improvement to that part of the educational system to which the strenuous efforts of the State should now be directed in a still larger measure than hithertofore. Funds set apart for education at the local level should be exclusively used for primary education and larger part of provincial revenues should also be used for primary education. Primary education should be extended in backward districts, e.g., those inhabited by aboriginal race. School curriculum should be adapted to the environment and should be simplified whenever possible. Practical subject, such as Indian method of arithmetic and accounts should be introduced. Instruction should be in the mother tongue of the children. The Government should assist the local funds by a suitable system of grants-in-aid."

Secondary Education

The Despatch recommended that at least one model high school be established in such districts, where these be required in the interests of the people, and the people themselves may not be advanced or wealthy enough to establish such schools for themselves and these be assisted with a grants-in-aid. In the upper classes of high schools, there be two divisions: one leading to the entrance examination of the university, the other of a more practical character, intended to fit youths for commercial or non-literary pursuits.

University Education

It was stated in the Despatch that:

> "the rapid spread of a liberal education among the natives of India since that time the high attainments shown by the native candidates for Government scholarships and by native students in private institutions for the success of the Medical College and the requirement of an increased European and Anglo-Indian population have led us to the conclusion that time is now arrived for the establishment of universities in India."

It was recommended to establish universities on the model of London University. Each university was to have a Chancellor, Vice-Chancellor and syndicate. University budget was to be controlled by senate. University was to conduct examination and confer degrees. Affiliation was to be given to the colleges. No religious subject was to be prescribed in Degree examination. Law, civil engineering and various branches of knowledge were to be started. Professorships were to be constituted to deliver lectures. One university was to be established each in the presidencies of Bombay, Calcutta and Madras.

Private Education Institutions

They were to be run by local managing committees; these might charge fees, but the accounts were to be open for inspection by Government officers of the education department. The Government was to provide grants-in-aid of teachers' salaries, buildings, libraries and scholarship.

Medium of Instruction

The Despatch said that:

> "in any general system of education, English language should be taught where there is a demand for it; but such instruction should always be combined with a careful attention to the study of the vernacular language of the district, and with such general instruction as can be conveyed through that language; and while the English language continues to be made use of as by far the most perfect medium for the education of those persons who have acquired a sufficient knowledge of it to receive general instruction through it.... We look, therefore, to the English language and to the vernacular languages of India together as media for the diffusion of European knowledge...."

Grants-in-Aid

The follwing extracts from the Despatch lay a basis for the grants-in-aid:

> "...the most effectual method of providing for the wants of India in this respect will be to combine with the agency of the Government the aid which may be derived from the exertion and the liberality of the educated and wealthy natives of India, and other benevolent persons."

Furthermore the Despatch recounted the system of grants-in-aid in England and stated: "we have therefore resolved to adopt in India the system of grant-in-aid which has been carried out in this country with very great success; and we confidently anticipate by thus drawing support from local resources, in addition to contribution from the State and far more rapid progress of education than would follow a mere increase of expenditure by Government; while it possesses the additional advantage of fostering a spirit of reliance upon the local exertions and contribution for local purpose, which in itself is of no mean importance to the well-being of a nation."

The sledge-hammer seems to have fallen in the remarks of the Despatch which stated that :

> "we look forward to the time when any general system of education entirely provided by Government may be discontinued...and when many of the existing Government institutions, especially those of the higher order, may be safely closed or transferred to the management of local bodies under the control of and aided by the State."

The net result of the system of grants-in-aid of education was that the beneficiaries were the Christian missions as they ran the types of schools which were eligible for the grants.

Teacher Training

Before the arrival of the Despatch, there were no arrangements for teacher training. The Despatch recommended the establishment of at least one training college in each province. Further, it recommended trained teachers for subjects like engineering, medicine, law and other professional subjects. The Despatch observed that the students should receive stipends and trained teachers given salaries. Probably, there were hardly any funds for stipends and salaries, but the idea of teacher training was mooted.

Women Education

The Despatch stated that: "the importance of female education in India cannot be over-rated; and we have observed with pleasure the evidence which is not afforded of an increased desire on the part of the many of the natives of India to give a good education to their daughters...schools for females are included among those to which grants-in aid may be given...the Government ought to give to the native female education in India its frank and cordial support."

Mass Education

The Despatch took note of the fact that masses of the people could not obtain useful knowledge on their own. Thus, "we desire to see the active measure of Government more especially directed for the future of their object for the attainment of which we are ready to sanction a considerable increase of expenditure."

By establishing primary schools, middle schools and high schools, the masses had excess to education and *Macaulay's* downward filtration policy of education proved a flop.

Religious Education

The Despatch observed that Government and Government-aided institutions were secular but the pupils were free to consult the Bible, placed in the libraries of colleges and schools. Furthermore, it stated that: "this is as it should be; and we have no desire to prevent, or discourage any explanations which the pupils may, of their own free will, ask from the masters upon the subject of Christian religion provided that such information be given out of school hours." Such instruction was entirely voluntary on both sides.

Vocational Education

Vocational education was to be given through schools and colleges, established for the purpose. Perhaps, such a provision was to forestall the unemployment situation which was conducive to discontent and also to give an impression of benevolence of the British Government. The Despatch stressed that the purpose of education was to develop human qualities for success in life.

Administration of Education

The Despatch recommended the constitution of department of public instruction in each province (Bengal, Madras, Bombay, North-Western Province and Punjab) under a Director who was to be assisted by a Deputy Director and Inspectors. It was the responsibility of the Director to submit an annual report about education in his province.

Impact of the Despatch

The Despatch was adopted and the following steps were taken by the Government:

(*i*) Departments of Education were established in all five provinces.

(*ii*) Universities were established at Bombay, Calcutta and Madras.

(*iii*) There was increase in grants-in-aid.

(*iv*) The Government continued to be a partner in education.

(*v*) The first war of independence in 1857 made the Company divert resources to ensure its safety.

(*vi*) The British Crown assumed the responsibility of Indian Government in 1858.

(*vii*) Religious neutrality was observed strictly.

(*viii*) Structure of schooling—primary, middle, secondary, university—was established, laying the foundation of a system.

(*ix*) Education developed fast between 1858 and 1882.

Evaluation

To evaluate minutely a document of 100 clauses is not an easy task. Nevertheless, the main issues in the Despatch have been examined for their merits and demerits.

Merits

(*i*) It was for the first time that the Directors of the East India Company decided on a somewhat coherent policy on education. Comments on the aims of education have already been made earlier in this chapter.

(*ii*) Education in the doldrums of the Company felt the wind of change and the British Government was made responsible for the education of the people of India.

(*iii*) The "downward filtration theory" got blocked with its own sediments, when steps were taken to build an educational pyramid—primary, secondary, higher. Provisions for mass education, women education and vocational education further chocked the filtration process.

(*iv*) The Despatch recognized that no culture could displace the indigenous culture. Thus, the Indian languages alongwith English were to be the media of instruction.

(*v*) The system of grants-in-aid facilitated the growth and development of institutions in general but particularly those run by the Christian missions. After all, these missions were educating Indian children.

(*vi*) By mooting the idea of teacher training for which highly educated persons were to be selected, and by recommending better salary scales for teachers, the Despatch highlighted the importance of professional training and teachers' better image in the society.

(*vii*) The Despatch took cognizance of the need to maintain educational standards through the establishment of a Department of Public Instruction in each of the five provinces, with the Director, a Deputy Director, Inspectors and Deputy Inspectors.

Demerits

(*i*) *H.R. James* called the Despatch as "the Magna Charta of Indian Education". *M.R. Paranjpe* considered such a label "ridiculous" and *Nurulah* and *Naik* found "no justification" for the superlative terms.

(*ii*) The glorification of the western knowledge was so stupendous that Indian culture and philosophy required a microscope as well as telescope to locate them.

(*iii*) English was given—and acquired—a pride of place because preference was given in government service to those who had obtained qulifications through the medium of English.

(*iv*) "Secularism" was a double-edged weapon. It stopped teaching of Indian religions, but was comfortable to keep the Bible in the school libraries for consultation by the pupils.

(*v*) The system of grants-in-aid helped institutions which could raise fifty percent of resources—that is which were already reasonably well-off.

(*vi*) Administrative set-up caught the characteristics of "bureaucracy" which acquired a derogatory connotation.

(*vii*) Bookish knowledge was encouraged with a view to passing the examinations, acquiring qualifications and getting employment.

Conclusion

The *Wood's* Despatch infused some sense of direction into the educational venture—venture which was mired into oriental-occidental controversy; which was a victim of the indifference of the East India Company; which shivered with the emotional outbursts of *Macaulay*; and which tolerated the rubber-stamping by *Bentinck.* The Despatch has been glorified more than its real merits by some and criticized on a few points which, in fact, go to its credit. The merits of the Despatch appear to be more substantive than its demerits. At best we can call the Despatch a "blueprint" somewhat hazy though it may be or a "road-map"—to some extent, tortuous though it may be.

Points to Remember

1. The East India Company sent a Despatch in 1854, authored by *Charles Wood.*
2. The objectives of the Despatch were to diffuse the western knowledge, to raise the moral character, to provide manpower to the company and to take raw material from India to England and provide finished good to India.
3. The Despatch recommended a structure of education from the primary, through secondary to university stage.
4. It also made recommendations for women education, mass education, teacher training and vocational education.
5. A system of grants-in-aid was established.
6. The main merit of the Despatch is the establishment of a pyramid of education.
7. The main demerit lies in the non-implementation of many of its recommendations.
8. The Desptach is considered a landmark in the history of education in India.

EXERCISES

1. What was the educational situation in India before the *Wood's* Despatch?
2. Examine the objectives of education in the *Wood's* Despatch.
3. What were the recommendations on the structure of education—primary, secondary, university?
4. How did Despatch sound the death-knell of the policy of "downward filtration"?
5. What recommendations did the Despatch make concerning teaching profession?
6. Comment of the merits of the Despatch.
7. What were the demerits of the Despatch?

6

Lord Curzon's Education Policy

After the arrogance of *Macaulay* and its silent approval by *Bentinck,* the *Wood's* Despatch had a soothing effect. *Curzon's* statement, however, not only reminded the Indians of the sarcasm of his predecessors in authority, but also convinced them of British hauteur surfacing time and again: however, this time *Curzon's* slights generated national consciousness and created a demand for national education movement.

Lord *Curzon* was appointed Governor-General of India in 1899. He was well educated, efficient, bold and widely travelled in Asia. He understood the importance of India to the British empire. He brought about reforms in administration and Indian education. During his administration, he faced great famine, political unrest and social upheaval. For his derogatory remarks against Indians, perhaps, he has been rightly labelled as the "most hated" Viceroy by *Nurullah* and *Naik.*

Curzon's Education Policy: The Background

Curzon stated his purpose as the educational reform which he considered as deserving of prominent place in any programme of administrative reconstruction. The issues were:

(*i*) Because of the expansion of education through private efforts, the question of quality control was to be answered.

(*ii*) There appeared to be a *laissez-faire* situation in which institutions had mainly become coaching centres to pass the examinations.

(*iii*) A need was felt to organise some government institutions as models for private enterprise to emulate.
(*iv*) The British were considered as fit people to hold superior posts in Education Department.
(*v*) Schools were to be kept away from politics.
(*vi*) Education was to be controlled by the government and was to be improved.
(*vii*) There was a need to raise the standard of English language.

Gokhale and his supporters did not agree with the contentions, stated above and expressed their views as under :

(*i*) The slogan of quality first and quantity next had to be abandoned.
(*ii*) Control of secondary and university education by the British Government was to sabotage the growth of national sentiment.
(*iii*) Primary education was to be compulsory and there was to be expansion of secondary and higher education.
(*iv*) Education Department was to be completely Indianised.
(*v*) Modern Indian languages were to be adopted as the media of instruction.
(*vi*) Aim of education was to develop love for India and not for British rule.

The above views were reasonable, but were not acceptable to *Curzon*. He had his own views on education. He felt, so to say, to be a "lover" of education. In 1901, *Curzon* held a long conference at Shimla to which he had invited the Director of Public Instruction and Missionaries—no Indian was invited. Indians suspected the motives and rejected the recommendations.

Indian University Commission, 1902

Curzon was of the view that there was no change in university education because the universities had not followed the guidelines of London University. A Commission was appointed under the Chairmanship of Lord *Kailly* with two Indians—*Guru*

Dass Banerjee and *Syad Hussain Bilgrami*—as members. The purposes were to inquire into the conditions and prospects of the universities, make proposal for improving their constitution and working and make recommendations to elevate the standard of university teaching and to promote advancement of learning.

Recommendations

(*i*) Every university was to be a teaching university.

- (*a*) No college was to be allowed full privileges unless it was thoroughly well-staffed.
- (*b*) Teachers were always to be intimately associated with the government of the university.
- (*c*) The supreme governing body of the university was its senate which was not to be too large.
- (*d*) Senate and syndicate were reorganized: The members of the senate were reduced and their term was fixed as five years. The syndicate was to comprise between nine and fifteen members.

(*ii*) *Affiliated Colleges*: Teachers from the affiliated colleges were to be represented in the university senate. Proper arrangements were to exist in the colleges for teaching, and the rules for affiliation were to be strictly observed. Universities were to supervise the colleges.

(*iii*) *English Language*: Standard of English was to be improved by keeping classes small and by training the teachers of English by an Englishman.

(*iv*) *Other Languages*: Vernaculars were to be encouraged upto M.A. level and classical languages were to be studied for good mental training.

(*v*) *Examination*: It was found that teaching was subordinate to examination which was considered a necessary evil. There was opposition to appearing privately at the examination.

As Indians had turned against *Curzon* for his diatribes, they did not accept the recommendations. Also, the Commission did not deal with secondary education—a ladder to university education. Furthermore, the basic problems of university organisation were not addressed.

In spite of the opposition, particularly by *Gokhale, Curzon* got the main recommendations of the Commission passed by Imperial Legislative Council in the form of Indian University Act. The Act also included the main suggestions of the Government of India's resolution on Indian educational policy.

Indian University Act (1904): Main Provisions

As most of the recommendations of the Indian University Commission of 1902 were accepted, the main provisions were as follows:

(*i*) *Enlargement of Functions of University*: By giving the right of teaching together with the right to conduct examinations, the scope was enlarged. University could appoint teachers, encourage them to conduct research and promote discipline among students.

(*ii*) *Senate:* The number of members of the senate was fixed at the minimum of fifty and the maximum of one hundred.

(*iii*) *Syndicate*: The members of the senate got the right to elect members of the syndicate. The number was fixed as twenty, each for the universities of Calcutta, Bombay and Madras and fifteen each for other universities. The syndicates were given legal status and proper representation of professors was made compulsory.

(*iv*) *Role of the Government*: Although the British universities, by and large, had maintained their autonomy—protecting themselves both against the ecclesiastical and monarchical interference: in India, the Government secured the right to make laws, amendments and reforms, and give approval to rules, passes by the senate.

(*v*) *Recognition of Colleges*: The norms set for the recognition of colleges were made strict. The syndicate could cause the inspection of the colleges.

(*vi*) *Territorial Jurisdiction of Universities:* Earlier, some colleges had obtained recognition from two universities. The Act authorized the Governor General to fix the territorial jurisdiction of each university.

(*vii*) *Matriculation Examination*: Schools had to obtain recognition from a university, if they wished to present pupils at the matriculation examination.

Education Policy, 1904

Curzon was a lover of education, but it seemed that his love had a 'blind' spot, even it was not 'blind' altogether. He ignored all criticism by Indian nationalists and largely implemented the resolutions of the Shimla Conference. He declared his education policy on primary, secondary and higher education. Other features of the policy concerned religious education, education of woman and administration of education.

(*i*) **Primary Education**: *Curzon* felt that the government had not fulfilled its duty in regard to primary education and, thus, recommended education for the masses in the following fields:

(*a*) Teacher training institutions were to be established to train teachers for various levels of schooling.
(*b*) To make courses practical, agriculture education was to be given to teachers so that they could impart it to learners in rural areas and the subject of agriculture was to included in the curriculum of the schools.
(*c*) Physical education was to be compulsory.
(*d*) Kindergarten system was to be adopted.
(*e*) The grants-in-aid system, based on the examination results, for paying salaries of teachers was introduced. Raising the salaries of teachers was recommended. The contradiction between payment by results and increased salary was soon realised, and grant increased by 50 per cent. It was expected that there would be quantitative expansion and qualitative improvement. The former expectation was somewhat met but the latter was hardly met as there was illiteracy to be wiped out first. For example, the number of recognized primary schools in 1881 was 82,916, in 1901, it increased to 93,604 and in 1911-12, it rose to 1,18,262. The number of pupils was 2061541; 3076671; and 4806737 respectively. The figures related to some areas only.

Gokhale had been trying persistently to make primary education compulsory and free. His efforts were appreciated by the Indian National Congress and the Muslim League which separately passed resolutions for making primary education compulsory and free. *Gokhale* placed a bill in the Central Legislative Council for making primary education compulsory and free but government officials opposed it and the bill was not passed. Nevertheless, *Gokhale's* efforts brought about sufficient progress in primary education.

There was a change in the outlook of the British Government, and in 1911, the Emperor, *King George,* in an address to the Calcutta University, declared a grant of rupees one lakh for primary education in India.

(*ii*) **Secondary Education:** About the secondary schools, the policy document stated that "whether these schools are managed by public authority or by private persons, and whether they receive aid from public funds or not, the government is bound in the interests of the community to see that the education provided in them is sound...."

Schools were ranked as "recognized" and "unrecognized" —the former met certain criteria relating to demanding financial stability, management body, teachers and pupils. Unrecognized schools were those which did not meet the criteria. The worst part was to prohibit transfer of students from unrecognized to recognized schools, as such students were not allowed to sit the matriculation and upper secondary examinations and enter the universities. But on the public demand, more high schools were opened, and by 1922, the number of high schools rose to 7530 with 11,06,803 students.

(*iii*) **Higher Education:** Based on the recommendations of Indian University Commission (1902), *Curzon* passed an Education Act (1904) and made the following suggestions for improving university education.

(*a*) The rights of teaching, examining, appointing teachers, carrying out research, managing libraries and laboratories and planning how to ensure discipline among students were given to the universities.

(*b*) The number of seats in the senate was fixed at 50 as minimum and hundred as maximum. The term was for five years.

(*c*) The senates got the right to elect members—twenty each for universities of Calcutta, Bombay and Madras and fifteen for other universities.

(*d*) Syndicates were given legal status and professors were compulsorily represented.
(*e*) The Government reserved the right to reform and amend rules, framed by the senate and to make laws.
(*f*) Rules for the grant of recognition were made strict.
(*g*) Jurisdiction of universities was fixed.

(*iv*) **Religious Education:** No provision was made for religious education in government school, but non-government institutions were to make arrangements for religious education in accordance with each student's own religion.

(*v*) **Education of Women:** Free education with different curriculum was recommended. If there was a demand, separate schools for girls were to be opened.

(*vi*) **Education Department:** The Department was to facilitate the appearance of students in state examinations, award grants-in-aid and award scholarships to students of recognized schools.

Evaluation of Curzon's Contribution

Forgiving *Curzon* for his vilifications, *Naik* and *Nurullah* acknowledged *Curzon's* contributions to Indian education, but *A.N. Basu* felt that the way in which he wanted to reform raised suspicions in the minds of educated Indians as they suspected some deep political motive.

Conclusion

It may be said that *Curzon's* pill for curing educational illness was made of sugar, but he coated it with quinine: unfortunately, some quinine got mixed up with sugar and that was why, there were protests against his policy. However, credit should be given to *Curzon* in that his policies built a structure from primary to university, if not a system of education. He "knew what to do," but he did not acknowledge that many others also knew what to do—particularly, national leaders like Gokhale.

Points to Remember

1. Lord *Curzon* became the Governor-General from 1899. His tenure was full of controversies.
2. He wanted to ensure quality in education and wanted Government schools to be models for private enterprise.
3. The British were to hold important posts as they were considered superior to Indians. Standard of English was to be raised.
4. His views were opposed by *Gokhale* and other nationalists.
5. He appointed Indian Education Commission in 1902, which recommeded organization of universities on the model of London University.
6. In spite of opposition by the nationalists in India, he passed the Indian Universities Act, 1904.
7. Functions of the universities were enlarged.
8. He also recommended to increase the provisions for primary, secondary and higher education.
9. Inspite of his insults of Indians, he created a structure, if not a system, of education.

EXERCISES

1. What changes did *Curzon* bring about in education in India?
2. On what grounds did *Gokhale* oppose *Curzon's* views on education?
3. Examine the recommendations of Indian Education Commission, 1902.
4. What were the main provisions of Indian Universities Act, 1904?
5. Discuss the following statement:
"Curzon's education policy was a quinine pill coated with sugar"—Authors.

7

National Consciousness and National Education Movement

History has a forward movement. That is why what has already happened becomes "history". But history also keeps patience in that it can wait for events to take place as a consequence of certain words, actions, policies and programmes. The India-baiting by *Grant*, *Macaulay* and *Curzon* was bound to show its results and the growth of national consciousness and national education movements were the outcomes.

National consciousness was built into the psyche of soldiers, political and social leaders, writers, educationists and the ordinary run of children at school and their parents. The urge to master European knowledge through the medium of English of *Raja Ram Mohan Roy,* the first war of Indian independence in 1857, the organization of Indian National Congress in 1885, the partition of Bengal by *Curzon, Gopal Krishan Gokhale's* criticism of the British policies on education and the urge of the backward Muslim community to get education—all contributed to the upsurge of national consciousness and emergence of a national educational movement.

National Consciousness

Indians had never welcomed the British colonizers, but they in general and intelligentsia in particular could no longer tolerate insults by *Curzon* in his following statements:

- But undoubtedly truth took a high place in the moral codes of the West before it had been similarly honoured in the East: in fact, life in the West was solitary, nasty and brutish, when the *Vedas*, Buddhism and Islam preached and practised the gospel of truth.

- It was not the Indian intelligentsia but the British bureaucracy that spoke for the masses: it was far from the actual situation as the masses had no "love" for the British, although they might not have been as vocal and articulate as the intelligentsia; moreover, the British bureaucracy's patronizing attitude was to befool the masses.
- *Curzon* ridiculed journalists and politicians for not being capable of action: again his remarks betrayed the historical reality in that *Roy, Gokhale, Naroji, Tilak, Das, Ali brothers, Annie Besant* and many others could rightly talk of "we"—all Indians—the elite and the masses.

National Education Movement

As a result of national consciousness grew the National Education Movement, the main demands of which were:

(*i*) Indianization of the Education Department.
(*ii*) Appreciation of India's culture and civilization and promotion of these as components of world's heritage.
(*iii*) Study of western knowledge and science.
(*iv*) Inculcation of love for the motherland.
(*v*) Modern Indian languages and not English as the media of instruction.
(*vi*) Aims of education to promote self-respect and openness of mind.
(*vii*) Development of vocational education.
(*viii*) Economic development of the country.

Impact of Movement

All that nationalists wished for might not have happened, but there were noticeable achievements. For example, as observed by *P. Sitaramayya*, the National University of Aligarh, the Gujarat Vidyapeeth, the Bihar Vidyapeeth, the Kashi Vidyapeeth, the Bengal National University, the Tilak Maharastra Vidyapeeth and a large number of national schools of all grades, with thousand of students on the rolls, were started in all parts of the country...."

Gokhale was a member of the Imperial Legislative Council. In 1910, he moved the following resolution: "That this Council recommends that a beginning should be made in the direction of making elementary education free and compulsory throughout the country, and that a mixed commission of officials and non-officials be appointed at an early date to frame definite proposal."

Gokhale introduced Bills during 1910 and 1912 which aimed at free and compulsory primary education, appointment of a secretary to organize, supervise and look after primary education and establishment of a separate department in the Central Government to draw up a scheme for the expansion of primary education and sharing of the cost of primary education by provincial Government and local bodies in the ratio of 2:1. Government assured *Gokhale* that it was to consider seriously his resolution: he withdrew it. Much later, only three of his proposals were accepted, but not the main proposal—the heart of matter relating to primary education.

Gokhale was a fighter and he introduced another Bill, again focusing on free and compulsory education: the Bill was rejected but its impact on the thinking of the Government in India was felt and the Government launched a new education policy in 1913.

Government Resolution on Educational Policy, 1913

The main provisions of the resolution were:

(*i*) Lower primary schools were to be expanded and in addition to the three R's, subjects like village map, nature study and physical exercises were also to be taught. The status of lower primary schools was to be raised to the status of upper primary schools. If needed, more upper primary schools were to be opened.

(*ii*) Local boards were to be established in place of private aided schools. The *maktabs* and *pathshalas* were to be adequately subsidized. Inspection and management of private schools were to be made more efficient.

(*iii*) In urban schools, geography was to be taught and excursions organized.

(*iv*) Teachers were to be drawn from the same class to which students belong. They were to hold the qualification obtained after passing the vernacular middle examination and they were to receive one year's training. A trained teacher was to get a salary of not less than Rs. 12/- per month. There were provisions for his increment in salary, provident fund and pension. The number of students under one teacher was generally to range between 30 and 40—but not more than 50 students.

(*v*) The conditions of middle or vernacular secondary schools were to be improved and their number increased. Schools were to be housed in spacious and sanitary buildings which were to be inexpensive.

(*vi*) Suggestions were made for special utilitarian curriculum for girls. There was to be increase in women teachers and inspectors. Importance of examinations in the education of girls was de-emphasised.

(*vii*) Existing State institutions were to continue as models and grants to private institutions were to be proper.

(*viii*) The resolution provided for the expansion in university education. University and high schools were to be assigned different spheres of activities—high school were to be under the provincial government. The outbreak of First World War inhibited the full implementation of the policy.

Conclusion

In 1920-22, *Gandhiji* preached boycott of government schools and colleges. Indian National Congress wanted to start national institutions and these were started, but vis-a-vis the violence that erupted, *Gandhiji* withdrew from the movement and gradually it lost its tempo. Yet, it did not die. Two decades of beginning of the twentieth century were indicative of shape of things to come.

Points to Remember

1. The insults to Indians by *Grant, Macaulay* and *Curzon* aroused national feelings.
2. Some events like the first war of independence in 1857, organization of Indian National Congress in 1885 and *Gokhale*'s persistent criticism of British policies added to national consciousness and enhanced the urge for national education.
3. The demands were: to Indianise the Education Department, appreciate India's culture, learn western knowledge and sciences, adopt Indian languages as media of instruction and develop the country economically.
4. The impact of the movement was felt in that many national institutions came into being.
5. *Gokhale*, a member of the Imperial Legislative Assembly, introduced bills, supporting free and compulsory primary education. The bills were not passed, but these brought about some changes in the thinking of the Government.
6. In 1913 was passed a Resolution on Education which dealt with education from primary to university stages.
7. The non-cooperation movement against the Colonial Government and its institutions was initially supported by *Gandhiji*, but he withdrew when violence broke out. And the movement, though it had its impact, was weakened.

EXERCISES

1. Discuss any three insulting remarks made by *Curzon* against the Indians.
2. What were the demand of nationalists in the field of education?
3. Examine the recommendations concerning primary schools, embodied in the Resolution on Education Policy, 1913.
4. What were the main features of *Gokhale*'s Bills in the Imperial Legislative Assembly?
5. Why did the national education movement get weak?
6. What lessons do we learn from the events of the first two decades of the twentieth century?

8

Indian Education Commission, 1882

The war of independence in 1857 was a traumatic experience for the British empire in India. The Crown took over the administration of education from the Company. Queen *Victoria* was keen on maintaining peace in India. Moreover, the recommendations of the *Wood's* Despatch were not implemented and the Christian missions were sore with the Indian educational administration and agitated in India and England. A Commission under the Chairmanship of *William Hunter,* a member of the executive council of the Governor-General of India, was appointed to review the education policy. There were 20 members including Indian educationists like *Syed Mahmud, Anand Mohan Basu, P.R. Mudaliar, Hazi Ghulam, K.T. Talang, Maharaj Jitendra M. Tagore* and *Bhudeo Mukherji.* The Christian missions were represented by *Dr. Miller.* The D.P.I. of Mysore, *B.L.Rice,* was the secretary.

Terms of Reference

(*i*) "To enquire particularly into the manner in which effect has been given to the principles of the Despatch of 1854 and to suggest such measures as it may think desirable in order to the further carrying out of the policy therein laid down."

(*ii*) "The development of elementary education was the main object, contemplated by the Despatch of 1854....the principal object, therefore, of the enquiry of the Commission should be the present state of the elementary education throughout the Empire and the means by which this can everywhere be extended and improved."

Specific Issues for Consideration

(*i*) Should government withdraw from direct educational enterprise in favour of missionaries, as the Despatch of 1854 had created such hope?

(*ii*) What should be the policy of government about religious education? Should it be imparted in schools or not? If it was to be imparted, in what form and with what conditions was it to be imparted?

In addition to the above specific issues, the aims of the Commission related to primary education, role of the Christian missions and that of the government, grants-in-aid, and whether education was to be a pyramid. Any commission had to address itself to affairs concerning secondary and higher education.

Aims of the Commission

(*i*) To assess the position of primary education and to give suggestions for its reforms.

(*ii*) To evaluate the work of the missionaries in the field of education.

(*iii*) To find out if the government institutions should be allowed to continue.

(*iv*) To assess the ability of the grants-in-aid system. To find out the attitude of the government towards the private Indian enterprises in the field of education. To find out if they received encouragement from the government.

(*v*) The main purpose of the Commission was to study the problem of primary education and to suggest measures for its reforms. But the Commission also chose to look into the affairs relating to secondary and higher education.

It is interesting to note that the Commission worked hard for ten months, made several sittings, obtained opinions from the provincial governments, toured the country and produced a report of about 700 pages.

Important Recommendations

(*i*) **Indigenous Education:** It was recommended to make efforts to encourage indigenous institutions as they had survived a severe competition and had thus proved that they possessed both vitality and popularity.

(*ii*) **Primary Education:** The Commission observed for the State "to declare the elementary education of the masses, its provision, extension and improvement to be that part of the educational system to which the strenuous efforts of the State should now be directed still larger measure than heretofore."

(*a*) Primary education was to be regarded as the instruction of the masses through the vernacular for which State was to direct still larger measure than before and it was to be extended to backward provinces.

(*b*) The control of primary education was vested in the District and Municipal Boards.

(*c*) The indigenous schools deserved encouragement and incorporation in the official system of education.

(*d*) School curriculum was to be simplified to suit the environment and was to contain practical subjects. Instruction was to be given through the mother tongue of the learners.

(*e*) A specific fund was to be created for primary education. The funds for rural and municipal areas were to be separated. The local funds were to be assisted by grants-in-aid.

(*iii*) **Secondary Education:** (*a*) It was recommended to open at least one model high school in such districts where these were required in the interests of the people and provide them with grant-in-aid.

(*b*) The secondary schools were to be bifurcated—one division leading to the entrance examination of the universities and other more of a practical character, intended to fit youths for commercial and non-literary pursuits.

(*c*) Teacher training for secondary school teachers was emphasized.

(*iv*) **Higher Education:** (*a*) The grants to universities were to be determined by the strength of teachers and students, and need and capacity of the institution.

(*b*) The colleges engaged in higher education were to be given sufficient grants for experimental laboratories, reading rooms, libraries, equipments, science rooms, buildings and furniture etc.

(*v*) **Education Department:** (*a*) It was recommended to appoint local persons as inspectors.

(*b*) The number of inspectors was to be increased.

(*c*) The assistant inspectors were to receive better emoluments.

(*d*) Mostly Indians were to be appointed as inspectors.

(*vi*) **Religious Education:** (*a*) The Commission recommended that government was to have no hand in schools regarding religious education.

(*b*) The managers of the non-governmental schools were free to give or not to give a place to religious education. The government was to place no restriction.

(*vii*) **Women Education:** (*a*) Women were to receive education in subjects that their life demands.

(*b*) Education was to be provided by the local boards, or in their absence, by the government.

(*c*) The Commission recommended women teachers and inspectresses for girl schools.

(*viii*) **Muslim Education:** Muslim education was to be encourged through control by local bodies; medium of instruction was to be Hindustani; scholarships and freeships were to be awarded; and schools were to be inspected by Muslim inspectors.

(*ix*) **Missionaries and the Commission:** Commission observed that the missionaries were never to be given full control in the field of education as they could never win the sympathy and respect of the Indian people. However, they were allowed to follow their own independent course under the general supervision of the State and they were to receive all encouragement and aid that private efforts could legitimately claim.

(*x*) **Control of Education:** The Commission recommended that the government was to withdraw itself completely from the field of education.

Evaluation of the Hunter Commission

Merits

(*i*) The Commission focused on primary education and made recommendations for its improvement.

(*ii*) At the secondary level, it recommended the diversification of courses—literary and vocational.

(*iii*) It encouraged higher education through grants-in-aid.
(*iv*) Women education received some importance.
(*v*) The award of grants-in-aid was somewhat systematized.
(*vi*) It clarified the role of Christian missionaries as one of the organizers of education.
(*vii*) It encouraged indigenous and private enterprise in education.

Limitations

(*i*) The government being the most powerful agency of education was recommended to withdraw from the educational venture.
(*ii*) Primary education was entrusted to agencies which were not financially strong.
(*iii*) Recommendations on religious education were somewhat confusing and were not related to the situation in a multi-religious Indian society.
(*iv*) The recommendation on grant-in-aid, based on examination results etc., was not a healthy system, as had been seen in England and other British colonies of the period.
(*v*) Expansion of higher education vis-a-vis poor infrastructures resulted in dilution of standards.

Conclusion

The *Hunter* Commission appeared to have injected some vitality into the Despatch of 1854, but in fact it drained the vitality when the government shifted its responsibilities to the Boards. *Basu* said that "the financial resources of the Boards were going to be extremely slender and to expect them to do justice to their charge was to expect the impossible." However, *Nurullah* and *Naik* were of the view that "the historical value of this document (Report) was incalculable. The enquiry of the Commission led to great education awakening in India. In practical terms, the number of schools and colleges increased, but quality of education was adversely affected for want of funds. The champions of quantity, led by *Gokhale*, perhaps thought that quality would emerge out of quantity. Enquiry of the

Commission led to great education awakening in India." Number of primary schools in 1881-82 was 82916 and it increased to 93604 in 1901-02. Secondary schools increased from 3916 to 5724. Universities marginally increased from 4 to 5 but colleges more than doubled from 68 to 179.

Points to Remember

1. Indian Education Commission was appointed in 1882, with *William Hunter* as its Chairman. There were Indian members also.

   The Commission was to study how far the recommendations of the Despatch of 1854 had been implemented, particularly in relation to elementary education.
2. The Commission made recommendations on nearly all aspects of education.
3. It recommended encouragement of indigenous education.
4. Primary education through the vernacular was considered as mass education. Its control was vested in the District and Municipal Boards. The curriculum was to be more practical. Grants-in-aid were to be given separately for rural and municipal schools.
5. Secodary education was to be diversified into academic and vocational streams.
6. Grants were recommended for the universities and colleges.
7. There were to be Indian inspectors of education.
8. Government was to have no hand in religious education.
9. Women education and Muslim education were to be encouraged.
10. Missionaries were not be the sole controllers of education.
11. The Commission brought about education awakening in India.
12. There was lack of originality. There was a good deal of repetition of the views in the Despatch.

EXERCISES

1. Examine the background to the appointment of the Indian Education Commission of 1882.
2. What were the main recommendations of the Commission on primary education?
3. What did the Commission recommend for secondary and higher education?
4. Discuss the following statement:

"The *Hunter* Commission had a soft corner for Muslim and women education"—Authors.

5. What were the contributions of the *Hunter* Commission to the development of education in India?
6. Evaluate the limitations of the *Hunter* Commission.
7. Comment on the issue of quantity vs. quality in the post-Commission period.

9

Calcutta University Commission, 1917-1919

The recommendations of the *Hunter* Commission of 1882 brought about general awakening on education. *Gokhale's* persistence on increasing the educational provision at the baseline added to the growth of national consciousness and national education movement. *Curzon's* attitude of "I know what to do" about education resulted in Education Policy in India in 1913, claiming all round development of education. Against such a background, the government appointed a small but powerful commission in 1917, called the Calcutta University Commission. The Chairman of the Commission was Dr. *Michael Sadler,* the Vice-Chancellor of the Leeds University in England. Among other members of the Commission were Dr. *Gregory,* and Sir *Asutosh Mukherjee.* After its chairman, the Commission is also known as the *Sadler* Commission.

Terms of Reference

"To inquire into the condition and prospects of the University of Calcutta and to consider the question of a constructive policy in relation to the questions it presents."

Modus Operandi

The Commission examined secondary education as it formed the basis of university education. It also visited all university centres. After 17 months, it submitted its report in 13 volumes. The report was a critical as well as a comprehensive survey of issues and problems of secondary and university education. Its recommendations related to secondary education, University of Calcutta, all other universities in India, Muslim education, teacher training, technology, professional and vocational education and modern Indian languages.

Secondary Education

The Commission found that secondary schools were suffering from lack of educational tools and equipment and their outlook was narrow as they were influenced by public examination. The standards in the schools had fallen; they were not inspected periodically and were not given useful suggestions for improvement; and suitable subjects for intermediate classes were not included into the curriculum of the secondary schools.

Recommendations

(*i*) The intermediate classes were to be separated from the universities and only intermediate pass candidates were to be admitted to universities.

(*ii*) Intermediate classes were to be independent or with high school classes.

(*iii*) Subjects useful for practical life were to be compulsory. Science, art, agriculture, medicine, engineering and teacher training were to be included in the curriculum.

(*iv*) An independent board of high school and intermediate education comprising representatives from high schools, intermediate colleges, universities and the government was to be established in each province.

(*v*) The medium of instruction in the intermediate colleges was to be the mother-tongue.

University Education

(*i*) As the Calcutta University comprising affiliated educational institutions had become too over-sized to function satisfactorily, it was recommended to establish a university at Dacca.

(*ii*) The colleges within the urban areas were to be organized into one teaching university.

(*iii*) The colleges in the rural areas were to be organized into a university college.

(*iv*) Enough freedom was to be given for the university to perform its duties, with liberal and flexible regulations.

(*v*) The B.A. course was to be of three years duration.

(*vi*) For appointing readers and professors, outside experts were to serve on the selection committee.

(*vii*) The Vice-Chancellor was to be a salaried person.

(*viii*) A court of representatives was to replace the senate and an executive council was to replace the syndicate.

(*ix*) There were to be a board and an academic council. The board was to prescribe the curriculum, conduct examination, organize research work, hold convocation and award degrees. The academic council was to deal with problems relating to education.

(*x*) A director of health education was to be appointed to look after the health of the students.

(*xi*) A board for women education was to be constituted under the control of Calcutta University for preparing curriculum for women education. Women were to receive education in medicine and teacher training.

(*xii*) Universities were to be co-educational, but for the young girls, schools were to be opened.

(*xiii*) Departments of Education were to be created at the University of Calcutta and Dacca.

(*xiv*) Applied science and other allied subjects were to be included in the university course. Professional and vocational courses were to be started at the intermediate colleges and universities.

(*xv*) To co-ordinate the work of various universities, an inter-university board was to be established.

Impact of the Commission

(*i*) **Primary Education:** Demand for compulsory primary education was increasing and many provinces passed compulsory education acts.

(*ii*) **Secondary Education:** The number of schools increased. English remained as the medium of instruction. Vocational courses and training colleges for teachers were started.

(*iii*) **University Education:** The following universities were created: Mysore University, Patna University, Benaras Hindu

University, Aligarh Muslim University, Lucknow University, Dacca University, Osmania University, Allahbad University, Lady Harding College, Delhi, SNDT Institute, Poona, Bhandarkar Institute for Oriental Research and the Institute of Philosophy. The working capacity of Calcutta University was increased. It was engaged in teaching and research. Thus, quality of higher education improved. The Calcutta University became a model for other universities.

Evaluation of the Commission

Merits

(*i*) The Government accepted the recommendations.

(*ii*) Other universities also benefited from the recommendations pertaining to Calcutta University.

(*iii*) University became a centre of teaching, research and providing degrees after examinations.

(*iv*) The burden of secondary education was transferred to boards of secondary education.

(*v*) Residential universities were established.

(*vi*) Teacher training department came into being in the universities.

(*vii*) *Purdah* schools were opened and special boards of women education were established.

(*viii*) For *Basu*, the recommendations were most "comprehensive and authoritative"; for *Mathew,* the significance of the report was incalculable; and for *Naik* and *Nurullah,* the report helped in the creation of new universities.

Limitations

(*i*) Many new programmes were recommended, but these were found to be too ahead of the prevailing situation. For example, the Calcutta University was modeled on the pattern of Cambridge and Oxford, but conditions in India were different. Similarly, provincial board of education were much ahead of the times.

(*ii*) Speical education for the Muslim—and not for the backward classes—was likely to sow the seeds of communalism.

(*iii*) A dual system of education was created: teaching of intermediate colleges was done by the universities and control and inspection were carried only by the secondary boards.

Conclusion

The reactions of the bureaucrats of the colonial power to expert reports had been, by and large, negative, so was the case with the *Sadler's* Report. However, that the wind of change had started blowing became evident when the government accepted the recommendations of the Calcutta University Commission and tried to implement them.

Points of Remember

1. The background events to Calcutta University Commission, 1917-19 were the *Gokhale's* bills, the *Hunter* Commission report and the general educational awakening in India.
2. The chairman of the commission was *Michael Sadler* and the membership contained Indians also.
3. The Commission inquired into matters relating to the Calcutta University and secondary schools.
4. The recommendations made the Calcutta University a model for other universities which came into being thereafter.
5. Departments of education were created at Calcutta and Dacca.
6. Detailed recommendations were made in relation to the senate, the syndicate, appointment of readers, professors and the vice-chancellor, university autonomy, curriculum and women education.
7. Intermediate classes were to be taught by the universities, but controlled by secondary boards.
8. Applied science and other related subjects were to be included in university curriculum.
9. *Purdah* schools and special boards of women education were recommended.
10. The reports of the Commission helped in the creation of new universities.
11. The recommendations were rather ahead of the situation, prevailing then.

EXERCISES

1. What were the main recommendations of the Calcutta University Commission (*Sadler* Commission) on university education?
2. How did the *Sadler* Commission tackle the issue of secondary education?
3. Examine the recommendations of the *Sadler* Commission on women education.
4. Comment on the following statement:
   "The *Sadler* Commission report was a harbinger of university education in India"—Authors.
5. What contribution did the *Sadler* Commission make to education in India?
6. What were the limitations of the *Sadler* Commission?

10

Wardha Scheme of Education, 1937

Wardha scheme of education by *M.K. Gandhi* is also known as basic education, *nai talim, buniyadi talim,* and basic *shiksha.* But before the scheme, certain other events took place which are worth recognizing, however briefly. These are: *Hartog* Committee report of 1929; Government of India Act, 1935 and *Abbot-Wood* Committee Report, 1937.

The *Monto-Ford* (*Montogu-Chemsford*) politics introduced diarchy into provincial administration in the form of:

(*i*) the reserved and (*ii*) the transferred lists. Education was transferred to Indian ministers, but certain areas and institutions remained centrally administered. The Indian minister had no control over the subject of finance as it was treated as reserved. Moreover, the Governors had the veto power and there was a gulf between the top officers of the education department who were under the direct control of the Secretary of State and the Indian ministers.

Sir *Philip Hartog* Committee was entrusted the job of inquiring into primary education. In its report, the Committee pointed out much wastage and stagnation in primary education. It recommended a policy of consolidation in place of expansion. In secondary education, the report pointed out the wastage due to laxity in promotion from one class to other and prosecution of higher education by incapable students. It recommended diversified and varied curricula in the middle schools and the diversion of more boys to the industrial and commercial careers at the end of the middle stage. The universities were reported to have maintained a high standard of education. In the official circles, the report was hailed as the torch bearer of State efforts, but it was criticized in the non-official circles as a political device to check the expansion of mass education.

The Government of India Act abolished the diarchical system and introduced provincial autonomy. It divided all education activities into two categories—(*i*) Federal (or Central) subjects; (*ii*) State (or Provincial) subjects. Education matters others than those which were Federal were Provincial matters.

The authors of the *Abbot-Wood* Report (1937) were *A. Abbot* and *S.H. Wood—Wood* recommended trained teachers for primary schools and change in curriculum. *Abbot* highlighted the importance of vocational education.

Foundations of Basic Education

The propounder of Basic Education, *M.K. Gandhi*, wrote in the *Harijan* in 1937 thus:

> By education, I mean an all round drawing out of the best in child and man; child's education by teaching it a useful handicraft and enabling it to produce from the moment it begins its training. Thus every school can be made self supporting, the condition being that the State takes over the manufactures of the school.

The 1937 quotation sums up the philosophy, sociology and psychology of what *Gandhiji* meant to achieve through Basic Education. Philosophy concerns the aim of education, and it is complete development of the learner. Sociology relates to productivity of the learners which should be taken over by the State. Psychology is implied in the developmental tasks of the learners through the craft.

In October, 1937 itself, a Conference of National Workers was called at Wardha under the presidentship of *Gandhiji* and the following resolutions were passed:

(*i*) That in the opinion of this Conference free and compulsory education be provided for seven years on a nation-wide scale;

(*ii*) That the medium of instruction be the mother tongue;

(*iii*) That the Conference endorses the proposal, made by *Mahatma Gandhi*, that the process of education through some form of manual work, and that all other abilities to be developed or training to be given should, as far as possible, be integrally related to the central handicraft chosen with due regard to the environment of the child;

(*iv*) That the Conference expects that the system of education will be gradually able to cover the remuneration of the teacher.

For the preparation of a detailed syllabus, a committee of renowned educationists under the chairmanship of Dr. *Zakir Hussain* was appointed. The committee submitted two reports: one in 1937, the other in 1938.

The first report dealt with:

(*i*) Basic principles of the scheme:
(*ii*) Prevalent education system;
(*iii*) *Gandhiji's* leadership;
(*iv*) Craft in school;
(*v*) Stress on cultivation of the qualities of good citizenship; and
(*vi*) Self-supporting aspect of the scheme.

The second report covered:

(*i*) Basic craft—agriculture, metal work and carpentry;
(*ii*) Syllabus;
(*iii*) Methods of teaching;
(*iv*) Correlation of craft and other subjects.

The 1938 report was presented to Haripura Congress Session in Febuary, 1938 and criticisms were replied to by *Gandhiji*.

Salient Features of Wardha Scheme

(i) Child-Centred Education

When there were few books in the world of learning, education was teacher-centred. When a lot of reading material became available, learning became curriculum-centred. When the concept of child-centred education dominated the thinking in the western world, its reflection was also seen in India. *Gandhiji* expected teachers to understand the learner and develop him according to his natural propensities. It was through the craft that child was to learn through his experiences, which were to be pleasant. In fact, in the learning process, teacher, curriculum and learner are equally important—someone has to teach: man or machine or both; something has to be taught: facts, attitudes, values; some one has to learn: child, adolescent, adult.

(ii) Activity-Based Education

Credit for activity-centred education goes to *John Dewey.* Although *Gandhiji* is a prototype, it is also true that he knew what Dewey was practising in his school in the U.S.A. In basic education, "craft" is the centre of all activities.

(iii) Unity of Knowledge

Gandhiji's technique of correlation in which all subjects are related to craft ensures what an educationist like *Jaktat* calls "unity of knowledge". Unity ensures useful and practical knowledge.

(iv) Goal-Directed Education

By engaging in craft, the learner creates something. Such creation gives him satisfaction and happiness. These states motivate the learner to produce or create more, of superior quality and that which is useful. So learning is not a leap in the dark, but purposive. Creation and production are the results of goal-directed efforts.

(v) Economic Aspect of Basic Education

Gandhiji knew that ultimately even an academic type of education was also to enable the learner to be productive. But he considered "earn while you learn" more important. For him, the money earned through craft should meet the expenditure on education: "self support" is an important aspect of basic education.

(vi) Development of Personality

The spirit behind basic education is to develop the learner physically, intellectually, emotionally, morally, socially and aesthetically. Such harmonious development is possible through craft as the focus of learning and all other subjects correlated to it.

Curriculum of Basic Education

As learners in Basic Education were children between the ages of seven and fourteen years, curriculum designe suited them.

(i) Basic Crafts

Basic crafts chosen suited the general environment of the community. These crafts were:

(*a*) Spinning and weaving
(*b*) Carpentry
(*c*) Agriculture
(*d*) Fruit and vegetable gardening
(*e*) Leather work
(*f*) Any other craft suiting the local conditions

(ii) Mother Tongue

Gandhiji considered mother tongue as an important means of instruction of the child for emotional, cultural and social reasons.

(iii) Mathematics

Mathematics was important to solve numerical and geometrical problems which arose in connection with craft. Learners were to gain knowledge of business practice and book keeping.

(iv) Social Studies

The objectives of teaching social studies were to develop in the learner a broad human interest in the progress of mankind, an understanding of social and geographical environment, belief in a co-operative society, based on love, truth and justice, responsibilities and right of citizenship, social virtues and respect for religions.

(v) General Science

The objectives of teaching general science were to provide learners an intelligent and appreciative outlook on nature, habituate them for accurate observation and experimental attitude, to make them understand important scientific principles, and for application of science in the service of man.

(vi) Drawing

Drawing was to train learners in observation and discrimination of colours and forms, develop aesthetic sense, increase the capacity for tasteful design and decoration and develop the capacity for drawing of objects.

(vii) Music

Children were to learn walking and clapping rhythmically, and learn group singing of inspiring songs.

(viii) Hindustani

Hindustani was to be the *lingua franca*. Children were to realize that it was the most important cultural contact between the Hindus and the Muslims and they were to appreciate the richness and vitality of this language.

Other Aspects

- Boys and girls were to study the same syllabus upto 5th grade. Girls were to learn domestic science in 4th and 5th grades and advanced domestic science in 6th and 7th grades in place of basic craft.
- Teachers were to receive 3 years of long term training and 1 year of short term training.
- Methods of teaching were to be activity-centred. All subjects were to be interrelated and co-related to the craft.
- No religious education was to be imparted. Self-reliance was the greatest religion. By example of good character and behaviour, desirable ideals were to be instilled in the children.

Progress of Basic Education

- The *Zakir Hussain* Committee modified the scheme. The rules relating to self-supporting aspect were relaxed.

- After 1938, basic education was adopted in Central Provinces, U.P., Bombay and Bihar-Orisa.
- Vidya Mandir schools were started for teacher training.

In 1938 and again in 1945, the Central Advisory Board of Education (C.A.B.E.) appointed committees under the chairmanship of *B.G. Kher,* which recommended that the scheme was to be introduced in rural areas, and age range of compulsion was to be 6 to 19 years. Children at the age of 11 could be sent to other kinds of schools, the mother tongue was to be the medium of instruction, and no external examination was required. C.A.B.E. accepted many of the recommendations.

- In 1945, the scheme was renamed *Nai Talim* or New Education.
- The scheme succeeded in Bihar, Madras, Bombay and the tribal areas, but was opposed elsewhere.
- An assessment committee on education was appointed by the Government of India in 1956-57. It reported that the standard of education in baisc schools was not satisfactory.

The Estimate Committee on Elementary Education recommended opening of basic schools in urban areas also; the existing primary schools were to be reoriented towards basic education, and high standards were to be maintained in basic schools.

Evaluation

As there are involved sentiments, practical realities, politics and dreams of technicalisation of India, the evaluation of the scheme is coloured by all these considerations.

Merits

(*i*) The greatest contribution of *Gandhiji* to educational wisdom is the importance he gave to "craft". Education through craft is psychologically sound as it relieves the learner of the theory and abstractness of the academic type of learning. It is socially useful as all children learn through the craft and the prejudice between manual and intellectual work is removed. It is economically viable, though its productivity may not result in self-sufficiency. It is educationally challenging as there is integration of knowledge.

(*ii*) Activity-based curriculum involves the physical and the social environment, and the craft work.

(*iii*) Learning by doing is superior to other methods as it leaves more permanent impressions of knowledge on the learner.

(*iv*) The scheme stands for free and compulsory education, recognized as a fundamental right in an amendment to our Constitution in 2001. Many parents may be so poor as to be unable to pay for the expenses of schooling—compulsion is useful in a situation where parents may not understand the advantage of education.

(*v*) The aim of basic education is to achieve the all-round development of the child. Such a development is not an easy task. The traditional schools of educational philosophy do claim to achieve the all-round development but the accent is on intellectual or vocational development.

(*vi*) *Gandhiji* synthesized individual and social aims. He said that "a nation cannot advance without the units of which it is composed, and conversely, no individual can advance without the nation of which it is a part also advancing". Education aimed at making children ideal members of a democratic society.

(*vii*) *Gandhiji* insisted on—and put into practice—education through the mother tongue, when he suggested that: "I hold it to be as necessary for the urban child as for the rural to have the foundation of his development laid on the solid rock of the mother-tongue." He considered mastery of mother-tongue "the foundation of all education"—as a valuable means of social education while also instilling right ethical and moral values.

Demerits

(*i*) *P.S. Naidu* observed, "There are three aspects of human nature—congnitive, affective and conative. The Wardha scheme emphasizes the last aspect piously hoping that the student will willy-nilly get trained in the first through his training in the last. The middle aspect is completely ignored." Thus, the scheme is psychologically unsound.

(*ii*) In practical terms, it is not possible to correlate all the subjects to the craft. *Naidu* went to the extent of saying that it was absured to hang all knowledge from the peg of a single craft.

(*iii*) An editorial of *Educational Review* said that "with rapid industrialization of India, knowledge of science and mathematics may become more desirable than skill in handicrafts."

(*iv*) Even the heart and soul of basic education—the craft—has been attacked. *R.K. Singh* said that "students spend one third or half the time for craft work without acquiring any dexterity worth *speaking* of any craft."

(*v*) The severest ciriticism of basic education has been carried out by the four "Fs"—fad, farce, fraud, fallacy.

Conclusion

It seems *Gandhiji's* basic education, supported by the Congress governments at the centre could not become popular. The Education Commission, 1964-66 did recognize the movement of basic education as "a landmark in the history of education in India," but it called for the reorientation of basic education programme," and the concept of "work experience" was popularized. The resolution on national policy on education, 1968 did not use the term "basic education" and acknowledged the Education Commission's concept of "work experiences". Committees like the *Ishwar Bahi Patel* Committee, and the *Adiseshiah* Committee, used the term "socially useful productive work". The National Policy on Education 1986 and its revision in 1992 did not seem to have mentioned "basic education" in their texts.

In spite of the spate of criticism against basic education and its elimination from important documents, it has to be acknowledged that India has not produced any educational philosopher other than *Gandhiji.* His philosophy of education is eclectic in nature, but it tackles all the four important problems of philosophy—metaphysics, epistemology, logic, axiology. If there are limitations in *Gandhian* philosophy of education, such can also be identified in the leading philosophies of the western world like Naturalism, Idealism, Realism and Pragmatism. The thrust on vocationalisation of education in various policy documents must be attributed to the pride of place assigned to "craft" in the Wardha Scheme of Education. The scheme was a part and parcel of the multiconceptual approach to education and should have been given a place in the system of education in India. Such a policy would have been a great honour to *Gandhism* which has received enough of lip service from various governments in the country.

Points to Remember

1. Wardha Scheme of education, also called basic education, *nai talim, buniyadi talim,* was launched by *M.K. Gandhi* in the late 1930s.
2. Before launching of the scheme, there came the *Hartog* Committee Report 1929, Government of India Act, 1935, *Abbot-Wood* Committee Report, 1937 and *Mont-Ford* diarchy: all these concerned and affected education.
3. *Gandhiji* in 1937 stated in the *Harijan* the philosophical foundations of basic education.
4. A Conference of National Workers at Wardha in 1937 under the chairmanship of *Gandhiji* resolved to provide free and compulsory education for seven years through the medium of mother-tongue and it was to be craft-based.
5. The *Zakir Hussain* Committee worked out the detailed syllabus.
6. The scheme was launched in U.P., C.P., Bihar, Orissa and Bombay.
7. The syllabus included crafts, mother-tongue, mathematics, social studies, general science, drawing, music and Hindustani.
8. The scheme was child-centred, activity-based, goal-directed, economically viable, but it was criticised for being a fad, farce etc.
9. Basic education has influnced the vocationalisation of education and it should have been given a place in the system of education in India.

EXERCISES

1. Examine the importance of the resolutions at Wardha in terms of their importance to Basic Education.
2. What are the salient features of the Wardha Scheme of Education?
3. Does the curriculum of Basic Education prepare the learner as a useful citizen?
4. Discuss the merits of the Wardha Scheme of Education.
5. What criticism has been made of Warha Scheme of Education.
6. Why has the Basic Education programme virtually disappeared from the system of education in India?

SECTION–III

INDEPENDENCE AND AFTER
(*HOPES AND ASPIRATIONS*)

11

University Education Commission, 1948-49

"Education" is a serious matter and higher education is more serious, for it produces manpower for leadership in diverse fields of activities in a nation. Although before independence, the *Wood's* Depatch of 1854, *Curzon's* Education Policy, Indian Education Commission, 1882 and Calcutta University Commission, 1917 were concerned with higher education, yet after independence, it was the University Education Commission that grappled with the higher education in all its manifestations. But before discussing the Commission, a link with developments between Wardha Scheme of Education and the 1948-49 Commission needs establishing. A noteworthy event was the *Sargent* Report of 1944.

Sargent Report

The Central Advisory Board of Education appointed a committee under Sir *Jogindra Singh* as the Chairman and twenty two other members, *John Sargent* was the educational adviser to the Government of India, and one of the members of the committee. Surprisingly, the report is not known after its chairman, but the educational adviser as the *Sargent* Report.

The report observed that India would reach the educational standard of the England of 1939 in a period of not less than 40 years. The report made the following recommendations:

(*i*) An adequate provision of pre-primary instruction in the form of nursery schools or classes was an essential adjunct to any national system of education. Such schools were to be free and manned by women teachers.

(*ii*) A system of universal, compulsory and free education for all boys and girls between the ages of six and fourteen was to be introduced as speedily as possible. The senior basic school—the finishing school for the majority—was considered of fundamental importance.

(*iii*) For bright children, high schools were to provide a course for six years in academic and technical streams.

(*iv*) The intermediate course was to be abolished and university degree was to be of three years duration.

(*v*) The establishment of an efficient system of technical education at all stages was a matter of great urgency.

(*vi*) Provisions of facilities for adult education were to be made on the widest scale.

(*vii*) New teacher training colleges including university education departments were to be provided and no fees were to be charged.

(*viii*) Recommendations were also made on school medical service, education of the handicapped, female education, mother tongue as the medium of instruction, recreation and social activities and provinces to be the main units of administration.

(*xi*) Total annual expenditure was estimated to be Rs. 3126 million. *K.G. Saiyidain* considered the report valuable; *Syed Nurullah* and *J.P. Naik* criticized it for its tame objectives, financial carelessnesss and being based on the British ideas and pattern. Nevertheless, the *Sargent* report was a thought provoking document before the independence of India in 1947, when in 1948 was appointed the University Education Commission.

Composition of the Education Commission

Dr. *S. Radhakrishnan* was the Chairman and there were 9 members—Dr. *Tara Chand*, Professor *S.K. Sidhanta.* Dr. *James F. Dutt*, Dr. *A.L. Mudaliar*, Dr. *Meganand Saha*, Dr. *Karm N. Bahl*, Dr. *John J. Tigert*, Dr. *Zakir Hussain* and Dr. *Arhtur E. Morgan.*

The composition of the Commission was marked by people of high and diverse intellectual abilities and experience in higher education. Moreover, it comprised members drawn from relevant international spectrum of education—India, the U.K. and the U.S.A.

Terms of Reference

The Commission was to consider and make recommendations with respect to:

(*i*) The aims and objectives of university education and research in India.

(*ii*) The change considered necessary and desirable in the constitution, control, functions and jurisdiction of universities in India and their relation with Government, central and provincial.

(*iii*) The finance of universities.

(*iv*) The maintenance of highest standard of teaching and examination in the universities and colleges under their control.

(*v*) The course of study in the universities with special reference to the maintenance of a sound balance between the humanities and the sciences and between pure science and technological training and the duration of such courses.

(*vi*) The standards of admission to university course of study with reference to the desirabilities of independent university entrance examination and the avoidance of unfair discrimination which militate against Right 23(2).

(*vii*) The medium of instruction in the universities.

(*viii*) The provision for advanced study in Indian culture, history, literatures, languages, philosophy and fine arts.

(*ix*) The need for more universities on regional and other basis.

(*x*) The organisation of advanced research in all branches of knowledge in the universities and institutions of higher research in well-coordinated fashion, avoiding waste of effort and resources.

(*xi*) Religious instruction in the universities.

(*xii*) The special problems of the Banaras Hindu University, the Aligarh Muslim University, the Delhi University and other institutions of all India character.

(*xiii*) The qualifications, conditions of service, salaries, privileges and functions of teachers and the encouragement of original research by teachers.

(*xiv*) The discipline of students, hostel and the organization of tutorial work and any other matter which is germane and essential to a complete and comprehensive enquiry into all aspects of university education and advanced research in India.

The Modus Operandi

The Commission worked out a detailed questionnaire and sent it to 1000 persons; only 600 persons returned the completed questionnaires. Educationists, vice-chancellors, teachers and students were interviewed on the basis of observations of respondents. A report comprising 747 pages, distributed in two volumes was presented. The first volume contained 18 chapters and the second volume contained statistics of institutions and evidence of witnesses.

The report was submitted to the government on 25 August, 1949.

Recommendations

(*i*) *Aims and Objectives*: Perhaps very few reports on education laid down the aims and objectives so comprehensively as was done by the Commission of 1948-49. After combining the repetitions, the aims were as follows:

(*a*) The universities were expected to provide leadership in politics, administration, education, industry and commerce.

(*b*) The universities were to train intellectual pioneers of civilization.

(*c*) The universities were to produce intellectual adventurers, who would disseminate learning to make democracy successful through the realization of justice, freedom, equality and fraternity.

(*d*) One of the main functions of the universities was to bring about the spiritual development of students, but these were to develop students physically also.
(*e*) Universities were to give the most important place to mother tongue in general education.
(*f*) Education was to discover innate qualities of a person and develop them through training.

The objectives were individual as well as social; these were material as well as spiritual; these were related to the past as well as the present; and these were cultural as well as vocational.

(*ii*) *Teachers*: The Commission noted that teachers had no facilities for research and libraries, resulting in the lack of knowledge of their subjects. Teachers tended to interest themselves more in the administrative affairs of the universities than in their legitimate duties. The salaries of teachers were low; hence they had "no incentive to throw themselves heart and soul into their work." Thus, the Commission recommended that there were to be facilities of provident fund to which teachers were to contribute 10 percent of the salary and the university 10 percent. There was to be a provision of residential accommodation on rental basis in the neighbourhood and hostels. Ordinarily, teachers were to retire at the age of 60, but in case of proficiency, they could be allowed up to 64 years. A provision was also made for study leave. Their working hours were to be eighteen periods a week, including tutorials. Salary scales were also fixed: professors got 900-50-1350 per month—the highest, and instructors or fellows got Rs. 250-25-500 per month—the lowest. Scales of salaries in the affiliated degree and postgraduate degree colleges were low.

(*iii*) *Standard of Teaching*: Students were to be admitted to the university courses when they had acquired 12 years of study at school or an intermediate college. For raising the standard of education and teaching, large number of well-equipped and well-staffed intermediate colleges were to be established in each province. To divert students to various vocations, good number of vocational institutions were to be started. The universities were to organise refresher courses for the teachers of high schools and intermediate colleges. The number of students was not to go beyond 1500. The session was to be divided into three terms, each of 11 weeks duration. Lectures were to be carefully planned and supplemented by tutorial, library work and written exercises. Undergraduate students were to attend lectures compulsorily. Buildings and equipment were to be improved. Pass marks were to be 40 percent, second division started at 55 percent and first division at 70 percent.

(*iv*) *The Curriculum*: Courses were to aim at unity of knowledge and experience. Thus, general education was to aim at mastering wisely selected information as to facts and principles. The study of theory as well as practice of general education was to be undertaken both at the universities and the secondary schools. Next stage was of liberal education which prepared students for independent thinking, for critical enquiry and for creating the constructive thought and action. Occupational education prepared students for their life work or for other specialized interest, but the Commission suggested to do away with the overemphasis on specialisation.

(a) Course of study at secondary school level comprised:

- Mother tongue
- Federal language; for those whose mother tongue was the federal language, a classical or modern Indian language was recommended.
- English
- General science or social studies.
- Logic, psychology, science, home science, hygiene, mathematics, physics, chemistry, biology, elements of accountancy, book keeping, element of business method, economics, history, geography, stenotyping, industrial organization, commercial arithmetic, and elements of soil science.

(b) Course of study at the first degree level included:

- Federal language; for those whose mother tongue was the federal language, a classical or modern Indian language was recommended.
- English
- For arts students, not less than two subjects, preferably one from humanities and one from social studies.

- For science students, not less than two subjects from mathematics, physics, chemistry, botany, zoology and geology.

(*c*) At the postgraduate level, the students were to be trained in hard intellectual endeavour. Students for research leading to Ph.D. degree were to be selected on the all India basis.

(*v*) *Professional Education*: The Commission made valuable suggestions for providing education in agriculture, commerce, medicine, engineering, technology, law and teaching.

(*vi*) *Religious Education*: All educational institutions were to start working with a few minutes of silent meditation. Lives of great religious leaders of all religions were to be taught in the first year and some selections of the universal character of the scriptures of the world would be studied in the second year and later, the central problems of philosophy of religions were to be considered.

(*vii*) *Education of Women*: After observing that there cannot be an educated people without education of women, the Commission recommended that education was to make them successful and good housewives; they were to be given maximum facilities for education; in co-education institutions, due regard was to be paid to behaviour towards ladies; and their female teachers were to be given the same pay as the male teachers got.

(*viii*) *Rural Universities*: The Commission recommended the establishment of rural universities and rural colleges and an all-India institue of rural education. The aim was to provide general education to rural boys and girls and encourage them to go in for a curriculum of some professional or occupational institutions.

(*ix*) *Medium of Instruction*: The Commission suggested the teaching of English in secondary schools, colleges and universities as before: but it observed that in order to get the fullest benefit of the higher education, English as the medium of instruction was to be replaced by some other Indian languages at the earliest. Constructive steps were to be taken to develop regional languages and the federal language. This, by and large, implied the learning of three languages—English, Federal,

Regional. A uniform list of technical and scientific terms for all Indian languages was recommended.

(*x*) *Discipline*: The Commission observed that good discipline was an individual responsibility for behaviour. Indiscipline had many causes—personal, social, economic, administrative and so on. It recommended constructive approaches to the solution of disciplinary and allied problems, devlopment of social conscience, self-respect and self-reliance. Furthermore, it considered the National Cadet Corps as a useful form of developing discipline. The Commission recommended that students were not to be encouraged to engage in party politics. Co-operation of the parents, the political leaders, the public and the press was considered a "must" to ensure discipline.

(*xi*) *Finance*: The Commission recommended the setting up of a University Grants Commission to allocate finances to the universities but the State Governments were to shoulder the major burden of the university education. Recurring and non-recurring grants were recommended for non-government colleges.

Evaluation

The report of the University Education Commission was a comprehensive document, with more strengths and less shortcomings.

Merits

(*a*) In relation to secondary education, the Commission presented an original point of view in that the aims were to develop democratic qualities in students and build character and discipline.

(*b*) The Report synthesized the knowledge and wisdom of the East and the West and ancient and modern. *S.P. Chaube* praised the Report on this account.

(*c*) On the one hand, the Report laid emphasis on scientific thoughts; on the other, it warned against ignoring moral and spiritual values.

(*d*) The education structure of 10+2+3 was recommended, though it began much later in 1975.

(*e*) The Report brought out the significance of women education.
(*f*) Setting up of universities in rural environment was a unique idea.
(*g*) It 'enthroned', the 'deposed' teachers by highlighting the importance of their roles and by improvement in their salaries.
(*h*) Its recommendations on how to ensure discipline were very insightful and pragmatic.
(*i*) There was tremendous development in university education after the Report. *Naik and Nurullah* praised the unprecedented expansion.

Demerits

(*a*) Many recommendations were the follow up of previous reports. Thus, these lacked originality, expected of such a high powered report.
(*b*) The curriculum was burdened with three language formula—English, Federal, Regional languages.
(*c*) No clear cut distinction was made between the curriculum for boys and girls, although many of their requirements were different.
(*d*) There was no rationale behind difference in scales of salary of university and college teachers.
(*e*) If the entire Report was considered, it was more of a philosophical than a practical document.

Conclusion

The *Radhakrishnan* Commission was a landmark in the history of education in India, not only for its high-powered composition, but also for its insightful, comprehensive and forward looking recommendations. The Chairman and the Commissioners were distinguished people in variety of fields, who with their recommendations proved that they lived in a world of reality and not in an ivory tower. They looked "before and after" and left indelible marks "on the sands of time", which helped the succeeding commissioners and educationists to give forward movement to educational thinking and practice so that an educational system emerges in India.

Points to Remember

1. Before the University Education Commission, 1948-49, the attention engaging developments in education were the Wardha Scheme and the *Sargent* Report.
2. In 1948, the University Education Commission under the Chairmanship of Dr. *Radhakrishnan* and 9 other members was called upon to study university education in its totality in India and make recommendations.
3. The Commission submitted its Report in 1949.
4. The aims of university education were defined comprehensively—individual, social, political, economic, vocational, philosophical.
5. Teachers were recognized as important agents of education; their salaries were to be increased.
6. Recommendations were made to improve standard of university education.
7. The curriculum—arts, sciences, humanities—was elaborately described.
8. Religious education which was not focused on any particular religion was recommended.
9. Education of women was encouraged.
10. It was recommended to establish rural universities.
11. Three language formula—English, Federal, Regional—was recommended.
12. University Grants Commission was to be established to manage finances.
13. The Report was a landmark in the history of higher education. Its merits outweigh its limitations.

EXERCISES

1. Describe the aims and objectives of University Education Commission (Radhakrishnan Commission).
2. What recommendation did the Commission make about secondary education?
3. Examine the steps recommended by the Commission to improve standards of teaching.
4. Discuss the views of the Commission on the role of teachers.
5. What were the merits of the Report of the *Radhakrishnan* Commission?
6. Evaluate the impact of the Commission on the development of university education.

12

Secondary Education Commission, 1952-53

Various commissions and documents had addressed themselves to secondary education, but such exercises were, so to say, incidental to their main focus. For example, soon after independence, the University Education Commission, 1948-49 made recommendations on secondary education also. When C.A.B.E. recommended the appointment of a commission to deal particularly with secondary education, the Secondary Education Commission was appointed in 1952.

Membership

Dr. *A.L. Mudaliar*: Vice-Chancellor, Madras University—Chairman.

John Christie: Principal, Jesus College, Oxford—Member.

Dr. *V.R. Williams*: Associate Director, Southern Regional Education Board, Atlanta, U.S.A.—Member.

Mrs. *Hansa Mehta*: Vice-Chancellor, Baroda University—Member.

Dr. *K.L. Shrimali*: Principal, Vidya Bhavan Teacher's Training College, Udaipur—Member.

Shri *M.T. Saiyidain*: Joint Secretary to the Government of India, Ministry of Education—Member.

A.N. Basu: (Ex. Officio Member) Prinicipal, Central Institute of Education, Delhi—Member-Secretary.

Dr. *S.M.S. Chari*: Education Officer, Minister of Education—Assistant Secretary, Seventeen member were-co-opted, one from each State.

The Commission came to be known as the *Mudaliar* Commission after its Chairman.

Terms of Reference

(*i*) To enquire into and report on the present position of secondary education in India, in all its aspects.

(*ii*) To suggest measures for its reorganisation and improvement with particular reference to:

(*a*) The aims, organization and content of secondary education.

(*b*) Its relationship to primary task and higher education.

(*c*) The inter-relation of secondary schools of different type, and

(*d*) Other allied problems so that a sound and reasonable uniform system of secondary education suited to our nees and resources may be provided for the whole country.

Modus Operandi

The Commission used two popular but largely authentic methods of enquiry. The first was the preparation of a questionnaire dealing with various aspects of secondary education. The questionnaire was sent to education institutions, teachers and experts. The responses were tabulated to collect sufficient information. Secondly, the members of the Commision toured various parts of India and collected firsthand knowledge of the situation, issues and problems of secondary education. It presented a report of 250 pages in 1953.

Findings

The Commission pointed out the following defects in the secondary education:

(*i*) Secondary education was bookish, mechanical, uniform and stereotyped: it did not cater to the different aptitudes of students.

(*ii*) It did not develop desirable qualities of cooperation, discipline and leadership, needed for becoming useful citizens of the country.

(*iii*) The content was overcrowded; methods of teaching were not up-to-date and scientific. Subjects of social importance were not given due importance.

(*iv*) Students were prepared to enter the university but after completing education, they failed to secure jobs.

(*v*) The teaching profession did not attract the right type of persons due to defective method of recruitment. Teachers could not establish contact with students who were in large numbers. The emoluments of teachers were not lucrative.

(*vi*) There was lack of facilities for co-curricular activities, play and recreation.

(*vii*) The atmosphere at home was not conducive to supplementing learning at school.

(*viii*) Education was not in complete consonance with the need of life: students did not develop a proper insight into the life.

Recommendations

The *Mudaliar* Commission noted that many of the recommendations of the previous commissions had not been implemented. It wanted to see that its own recommendations were implemented. Thus, it divided them into short term and long term recommendations. It also highlighted the point that recommendations required a review, but these had to remain permanent over a definite period of time.

(i) Aims of secondary education

- development of qualities, essential for creative citizenship;
- formation of vocational efficiency;
- development of personality; and
- the training for leadership.

(ii) New Organizational Pattern

The Commission observed that it was now generally recognized that the period of secondary education covered the age group of about 11 to 17 years. Properly planned education, covering about 7 years, enabled the school to give a thorough training in the courses of study taken up by the student and also kept him to attain a reasonable degree of maturity in knowledge, understanding and judgement which would stand him in good stead in life.

(*a*) Education was to commence after a four or five years period of primary or junior basic education and was to include the middle or senior basic or junior secondary stage of 3 years and the higher secondary stage of 4 years. The existing high schools and the higher secondary schools were to function on the lines laid down during the transitional stage. The intermediate stage was to be replaced by the higher secondary stage which was to be of four years duration—one year of the intermediate included in it.

(*b*) The first degree course in the university was to be of three years duration. Admission to professional colleges was to be opened to those who had completed the higher secondary course or had taken the one year pre-university course in the degree or professional colleges.

(*c*) Multipurpose schools were to be established to provide varied courses of interest to students with diverse aims, aptitudes and abilities. Those who had successfully completed such courses were to be given opportunities to take up higher specialized courses in polytechnics or technological institutions.

(*d*) All States were to provide special facilities for agricultural education in rural schools. Such courses were to include horticulture, animal husbandary and cottage industry.

(*e*) Speical criteria for converting high schools into higher secondary school related to accommodation, equipment, qualification of the staff, salaries and grades, and the provision of adequate finances.

(iii) The Issue of Languages

The Commission recommended a study of groups of languages—

(*a*) Mother tongue
(*b*) Regional language when it was not the mother tongue.
(*c*) Official or federal language.
(*d*) Classical languages—Sanskrit, Arabic, Persian, Latin etc.

(*e*) English as an international language.

(*f*) At the secondary stage, the medium of instruction was to be either the mother tongue or the regional language.

(*g*) As Hindi had been adopted in the Constitution as the official language of the Centre, it would become a means of communication of the people and of official correspondence between the Central Government and the States. Hindi would promote national unity and solidarity.

(*h*) If English were to be removed from the curriculum of secondary schools, its effects would be harmful for India.

(iv) Curriculum

(*a*) The Commission found the curriculum of secondary school as narrow, bookish, lacking in the power to develop the whole personality of the child and much dominated by examination.

(*b*) The Commission touched upon the principles of curriculum construction as totality of experience: variety and elasticity, core subjects, link with community life, the use of leisure and interrelation of subjects.

(*c*) Scheme of curriculum of the middle or senior basic school was to include English, social studies, general science, mathematics, art and music, craft and physical education.

(*d*) Curriculum at the high and higher secondary schools was to include compulsory subjects like mother tongue or regional language, course of the mother tongue and of a classical language, one other language to be chosen from Hindi for those whose mother tongue was not Hindi, elementary English for those who had not studied English in the middle stage, advanced English for those who had studied English at an earlier stage, a modern Indian language other than Hindi, a modern foreign language, other than English and a classical language. Social studies were to be for the first two years only.

General science including mathematics for two years only.

One craft to be chosen from ten areas—spinning and weaving, woodwork, metal work, clay modelling etc.

The optional subjects were to be taken from seven groups: humanities, science, technical subjects, commercial subjects, agricultural subjects, fine arts, home science (specially for girls).

(v) Text books

The Commission recommended a high-powered, independent textbook committee with the purpose of improving the quality of textbooks. The committee was to lay down clear criteria for the sale of paper, illustration, printing and format of the book. Textbooks as well as books of general reading were to be of quality. The amount realized from the sale of publications was to constitute a fund which could be utilized for awarding scholarships and providing books and other amenities for school children. Frequent changes in textbooks and other books were to be discouraged.

(vi) Methods of Teaching

Imparting of knowledge in an efficient manner was to be complemented by inculcating in the students desirable values and proper attitudes and habits of work. The principles of activity and project methods were to be assimilated in school practice. Teaching methods were to enable students to be trained in the techniques of study and self-study and to apply knowledge. A well-equipped library and subject libraries managed by trained librarians were considered essential for secondary schools.

(vii) Examination System

The number of external examinations was to be reduced by introducing objectives tests. School records were to be maintained to indicate the progress of each pupil. There was to be only one public examination at the completion of secondary school course.

(vii) School Administration

The Commission recommended the introduction of self-government in all schools. The house system with prefects or monitors was to be introduced. The students were to draw and enforce the code of conduct. Teachers were to provide education of character, keep close contact with students and direct extra-curricular activities. Religious and moral education was to be imparted on the voluntary basis after the regular school hours. A congenial atmosphere in the schools could ensure development of character.

(ix) Guidance and Counselling

The Commission observed that educational guidance was to receive greater attention. In order to improve pupils' understanding of the scope, nature and significance of various occupations and industries, films were to be shown. Trained guidance officers and career masters were to be appointed in secondary schools, and the government was to undertake the responsibility of opening centres for training them.

(x) Welfare of Students

All students were to be thoroughly examined medically every year and medical services were to be organised in all the States. Some teachers were to be trained in the principles of first aid and were to be given physical training. Teachers associated with physical training were to be able to teach subjects like physiology and hygiene. The training facilities were to be increased by expanding seats in the existing colleges and by opening new colleges.

(xi) Teacher Training

The methods of selection and appointment of the teachers were to be uniform throughout the country. In schools run by the private bodies, a committee including the Principal was to select teachers. As far as possible, only trained teachers were to be appointed, with a probation of one year. Salaries for the same qualifications were to be equal. Teachers in the high school were to be trained graduates and in the higher secondary school with qualifications as required for teaching in the intermediate college. A system of triple benefit fund—pension, provident fund and insurance—was to be introduced in all States. Physically fit and competent teachers were to be allowed to work up to the age of 60. Arbitration boards were to be established to look into appeals, grievances and disciplinary matters of teachers.

(*xii*) *Finance*

A close cooperation between the Central and State Governments was considered essential to improving the secondary education. An industrial education cess was to be levied and utilized for the furtherance of technical and vocational education at the secondary stage. Furthermore, railways, communications and posts and telegraph etc., were to make available a certain percentage of their net revenue for the promotion of technical education. The State Governments and the Centre were to assign lands to schools for playgrounds, buildings or agricultural farms without any charge. The Centre was to assume a certain amount of direct responsibility for the recognized secondary education and give financial aid for the purpose.

Evaluation

The *Mudaliar* Commission generated a good deal of interest in matters educational, particularly at the second level of education.

Merits

(*i*) The *Mudaliar* Commission reviewed the work of the past committees and commissions and it adopted their viable recommendations that suited an independent India.

(*ii*) By stating the educational aims as the development of personality, democratic citizenship, vocational efficiency and qualities of leadership, the Commission focused on general, vocational, political, social and psychological areas.

(*iii*) The recommendations of the Commission to provide the secondary education according to age, ability and aptitude was psychologically sound.

(*iv*) The idea of providing education and vocational guidance was not new to the world of learning, but it was somewhat new to the Indian system.

(*v*) By recommending experimental and activity-based

methods of teaching, the Commission revolutionized pedagogy which was otherwise mainly "chalk and talk"-based.

(*vi*) The recommendations on cumulative records was educationally useful as a history of the learner.

(*vii*) Industrial educational cess was desirable to make institutions financially sound.

(*viii*) That teachers were the most important agents in the scheme of education was appreciated and their recruitment, training, salary and other benefits, and apparatus for grievance redressal were favourably dealt with.

(*ix*) The introduction of objective tests was one of the modern methods of evaluation.

(*x*) The recommendation on the welfare of students through medical check up was rightly placed.

Limitations

(*i*) There was repetition of recommendations of the previous committees and commissions which was a limitation to the originality by the Commission.

(*ii*) The Commission left the blue-print incomplete in that no programme of action—short term, long term—was suggested, although recommendations were termed as short-term and long-term.

(*iii*) The Commission did not give much thought to the finanical aspects of the recommendations.

(*iv*) The multipurpose school did harldy benefit either the school learners or those seeking higher education.

(*v*) No strict guidelines were laid down for conversion of high schools into higher secondary schools. Social and political pressures succeeded in upgrading schools which did not satisfy the criteria.

(*vi*) The Commission did not consider the various aspects of the education of women.

(*vii*) English continued to be given importance and no clearcut language formula was suggested.

(*viii*) No concrete suggestions were made regarding the privately-managed schools.

Conclusion

It is worthwhile quoting *Bhagwan Dyal* who said that "if most of the suggestions of the Commissions are carried out, Secondary Education in the country will no doubt be placed on a healthy footing, where planned development will be possible in the interest of the country as whole." The point made in *Bhagwan Dyal's* quotation is valid even today. Many policies are worked out, but they fall short of implementation. The situation worsens in a unsettled multi-party democracy, where for narrow interests, the party or alliance in power may ignore the worthwhile work done by the opposition when it was in power: opposition is not treated as a component of the political system: at best, it is treated as an adversary and at worst, as an 'enemy'.

Points to Remember

1. Secondary Education Commission was appointed in 1952 and submitted its report in 1953.
2. Its Chairman was Dr. *A.Z. Mudaliar*; there were eight other members and secretaries, and 17 members—one for each State—were co-opted.
3. It was to enquire into and report on secondary education.
4. It recommended primary school of 4 or 5 years, junior secondary school of 3 years and higher secondary school of four years. First degree course was to be of 3 years.
5. It recommended study of groups of languages.
6. The curriculum was to be constructed on the principle of totality of experience of learners, variety, elasticity and use of leisure.
7. The quality of textbooks was to be improved.
8. Techniques of study, self-study and application of knowledge were recommended.
9. Self-governance was recommended in all secondary schools.
10. Guidance and counselling, and medical examination of students were recommended.
11. Trained teachers were to be preferred.
12. Cooperation between Central and State Governments in financial matters was recommended.

EXERCISES

1. What recommendations did the Secondary Education Commission (*Mudaliar* Commission) make about the aims of secondary education and what was new in the aims?
2. Discuss the recommendations of the *Mudaliar* Commission regarding the reorganization of secondary education.
3. Examine the recommendations of the *Mudaliar* Commission on the curriculum.
4. How has the country benefited from the recommendations of the *Mudaliar* Commission?
5. What were the merits of the *Mudaliar* Commission?
6. Discuss the limitations of the *Mudaliar* Commission?

13

National Education Commission, 1964-66

The history of education commissions in India from 1902 to 1966 is like a river, the course of which passes through falls, eddies, currents, subterranean movements and somewhat of a normal flow. One wonders if *Curzon* named Indian University Commission of 1902 as "Indian" in a derogatory sense vis-a-vis "British" or he did so with good intentions. After independence, the *Radhakrishnan* Commission of 1948-49 focused mainly on university education and the *Mudaliar* Commission of 1952-53 on secondary education. The brief of the National Education Commission 1964-66 was broad in that it directed its attention on all aspects of education.

Composition

Chairman—Dr. *D.S. Kothari*, Chairman University Grants Commission.

Member Secretary—*J.P. Naik*, Head of the Department of Educational Planning, Administration and Finance, Gokhale Institute of Politics and Economics, Poona.

The Commission had an associate secretary and there were 14 members. The membership included distinguished personalities both Indians and foreigners. Among the foreigners were *S.A. Shumovsky* (USSR), *M. Jean Thomas* (UNESCO), *Roger Revelle* (USA) etc.

Terms of Reference

"The Commission will advise Government on national pattern of education and on the general principles and policies for the development of education at all stages and all its aspects. It need not, however, examine problems of medical and legal education, but such aspects of their problems as are necessary for its comprehensive enquiry may be looked into."

Modus Operandi

The Commission went round all the States and selected Union Territories for about hundred days and visited universities, colleges and schools. It discussed matters concerning education with educationists, administrators, teachers and students. Two conferences of the representatives of university students were convened with a view to obtaining information about the problems in academic and welfare areas. Industrialists, scientists, reputed scholars and persons interested in education were interviewed. As many as 9000 persons were interviewed. In addition, memoranda, written reports and replies to the questionnaire were collected. There were over 2400 memoranda and notes. Seminars, conferences and special studies were conducted. The Commission called on the President, Vice-President, Prime Minister and Minister for Education and benefited from discussions with them. Task forces and working groups were appointed on various aspects of education.

The Commission started work on October 1, 1964 and submitted its report on June 29, 1966. The total expenditure on the Commission was Rs. 15,09,185.16.

Body of the Report

The report was divided into four parts. The first part dealt with educational and national objectives, the education system—structure, the standards, teacher's status, teacher's education, enrolment and manpower and equalization of educational opportunities. The second part discussed school education—problem of expansion, school curriculum, teaching methods, guidance and evaluation, school education, administration and supervision, higher educational objectives and improvement, the governance of universities, education for agriculture, vocational, technical and engineering education, science education and research, and adult education. The third part concerned the implementation of the recommendations—

educational planning and administration and educational finance. The fourth part contained supplementary papers and other relevant information of educational interest.

Major Recommendations

(i) National Aims

The Commission observed: "The present system of education, designed to meet the needs of an imperial administration within the limitations set by a feudal and traditional society, will need radical changes if it is to meet the purpose of a modernizing democratic and socialistic society... in fact, what is needed is a revolution in education which in turn will set in motion the much desired social, economic and cultural revolution".

(*a*) Education was to be related to productivity and national integration.
(*b*) It was to strengthen social integration and consolidate democracy as a form of government and help the country to adopt it as a way of life.
(*c*) It was to hasten the process of modernization; and
(*d*) It was to strive to build character by activation of social, moral and spiritual values.

(ii) Qualitative and Quantitative Programmes

The Commission identified three facets of educational revolution. These were:

(*a*) internal transformation as to the life, needs and aspirations of the nation;
(*b*) qualitative improvement so that the standards achieved are adequate, keep continually rising and, at least, in a few sectors internally comparable; and
(*c*) expansion of education facilities broadly on the basis of manpower needs with an accent on equalization of educational opportunities.

(iii) *Structure of Education*

For structure and standard of educational system, it was recommended that the educational pyramid required division into stages and their interrelationship, the duration of different stages, the quality of teachers, curricula, methods of teaching and evaluation, equipment and building and the utilization of available facilities.

(a) The new structure of primary education was to consist of:

- Pre-primary education—pre-primary, pre-basic, kindergarten, *Montessori*.
- Primary education—Class I to VII or I to VIII which included lower primary classes (I-IV) or (I to V) in some States, lower primary in some other States and lower elementary still in some States.
- Higher primary education—Classes V-VII or VI-VIII, middle in some States like Punjab, junior higher school in U.P., upper primary in Gujarat, senior basic, and higher elementary in Madras.

(b) For secondary education, the structure consisted of classes VIII-X or IX-X and named as:

- Lower secondary education—Classes VIII-X or IX-X: high school.
- Higher secondary education—Classes XI-XII—to include class XI or PUC in Rajasthan, junior colleges in Kerala, intermediate classes in U.P. and courses like pre-medical and pre-engineering in some other states.

(c) Higher Education

- Professional degrees: M.A; M.Sc; B.E.; M.B.B.S; L.L.B; etc.
- General degrees: All degrees other than professional ones.
- Under-graduate: All courses leading to the first degree.
- Post-graduate: All courses beyond the first degree (excluding certain first degrees given after the first degree. e.g., B.Ed.).

The Commission recomnendaded that universities and affiliated colleges were to have administrative autonomy.

(iv) Teaching Force

The Commission considered the professional preparation of teachers as crucial to the qualitative improvement of education.

They were to be brought into the mainstream of the academic life of the universities. Extension services departments were to be established in each institution's pre-primary, primary and secondary levels as an integral part of it. Comprehensive colleges of education were to be established in each State for teachers of different stages and fields. A State Board of Teachers Education was to be established in each State for making proper provision of teacher education at all stages.

Pay scales for teachers at various levels were fixed. Teachers who had completed secondary course and had received two years professional training were to start at Rs. 150 per month and reach Rs. 300 as selection grade. Graduates who had received one year's professional training were to start at Rs. 220 and receive Rs. 500 in selection grade. Teachers of secondary school having post-graduate qualifications were to start at Rs. 300 and reach Rs. 600. Teachers in approved affiliated colleges started at Rs. 300 as junior scale and reached Rs. 600. Senior scale started at Rs. 400 and reached Rs. 800. Senior Lecturers, Readers and Principal-I started at Rs. 700 and reached Rs. 1100, where as Principal-II ranged between Rs. 800 and 1250 and Principal-III received Rs. 1000 and reached Rs. 1500. Lecturers in the approved university departments ranged between Rs. 1100 and Rs. 1600. It was recommended to revise the pay scales, at least once in five years.

(v) Curriculum Considerations

The standards to be attained at different stages were to be defined in terms of the knowledge, skills, abilities and attitudes to be developed in relation to the overall objective of school education.

Lower Primary Stage (Class I-IV)

(*a*) One language—the mother tongue or the regional language.
(*b*) Mathematics
(*c*) Study of environment (covering science and social studies in class III or IV)
(*d*) Creative activities

(*e*) Work experience and social service
(*f*) Health education.

Higher Primary Stage (Class V-VIII)

(*a*) Two languages:
-Mother tongue or the regional language
-Hindi or English
-A third language (English, Hindi, or the regional lauguage) might be studied on an optional basis.
(*b*) Mathematics
(*c*) Science
(*d*) Social studies (or history, geography and civics)
(*e*) Art or craft
(*f*) Work experience
(*g*) Physical education
(*h*) Education in moral and spiritual values.

Lower Secondary Stage (Class IX-X)

(*a*) Three languages
(*b*) Mathematics
(*c*) Science
(*d*) Hisotry, geography and civics
(*e*) Art and craft
(*f*) Work experience and social service
(*g*) Physical education
(*h*) Education in moral and spiritual values.

Higher Secondary Stage (Class XI-XII)

(*a*) Any two languages, including any modern Indian language, any modern foreign language and any classical language.
(*b*) Any three subjects from
-An additional language
-History
-Geography
-Economics
-Logic
-Psychology
-Sociology

-Art
-Physics
-Chemistry
-Mathematics
-Biology
-Geology
-Home science

(*c*) Work experience and social services.
(*d*) Physical education
(*e*) Art or craft
(*f*) Education in moral and spiritual values.

The Commission recommended fewer holidays, increase in working hours, decrease in examination days, home work in long holidays and self study by using libraries, reading rooms, laboratories and workshops etc.

(vi) Teaching Methods, Guidance and Evaluation

In a dynamic, flexible and discriminating education system, the educational administration was to encourage and hasten the diffusion of new teaching methods by combining permissiveness with persuasion suggesting the employment of new methods, giving in-service training to teachers and providing adequate guide material, updated constantly.

Text books were to be produced at the national level. Teachers guides and other instructional materials were to supplement text books. Guidance and counselling were to be an integral part of education. At the primary school level, these were to familiarize teachers under training with diagnostic testing and the problems of individual differences. At the secondary stage, the services were to help in the identification and development of the abilities and interests of adolescent pupils. Teachers were to be introduced to guidance concept throught pre-service or in-serivce training.

Evaluation was related to educational objectives. The new approach to evaluation was to attempt to improve the written examination with a view of making it more valid and reliable. Internal assessment by schools was to be comprehensive and was to evaluate all aspects of the growth of learners, including those measured by the external examinations.

(vii) Equalisation of Educational Opportunities

Two types of inequalities were identified in the field of education: one was in the education of boys and girls; the second was in the education of developed and backward classes.

(*a*) In order to remove these inequalities, the Commission recommended that tuition fees at the primary level were to be abolished in all government, local authority and aided private schools before the end of Fourth Five Year Plan. Lower secondary education was to be free before the end of the fifth plan. For the next ten years, tuition fees at the higher secondary level and universities were to be free for the deserving and needy students.

At primary level, free text books and working material were to be provided. Secondary schools and universities were to develop book-banks and libraries were to store sets of text books for use of the students.

(*b*) At the primary stage, scholarships were to be awarded to a needy child; at the secondary stage, top 15% of the children were to get scholarships; at the university stage, scholarships were to be made available to at least 25% of the enrolments, and at the post graduate stage, the scholarships were to increase from 25% by 1970 to 50% by 1986. Scholarships were also recommended at the national level for vocational education and for study abroad. Loan scholarships were to supplement other scholarships.

(*c*) It was recommended to provide education to about 15% of handicapped children (blind, deaf, orthopaedically handicapped) by 1986 and to 15% of the mentally retarded ones. Teachers were to be trained to teach the handicapped children.

(*d*) Education for the scheduled castes was to be expanded. The nomadic and semi-nomadic people were to be provided educational facilities. Education of the tribal people deserved great attention and emphasis.

(*e*) Bold and determined efforts were to be made for the education of women. Special schemes and machinery were to look after girls education at the States and Central levels. Special financial help was to be given for developing education of the women.

(viii) Work Experience

An emphasis on work experience might be considered an innovation of the Commission. The programme of action was to begin with simple hand work, which was to develop emotionally and intellectually children of lower classes of the primary school. In the senior classes, a craft could be taught to develop technical thinking and creative capacities. Work on the farm and in the family could provide some work experience. Work experience of the lower secondary level was to take the form of workshop training—a workshop was proposed to be attached to every school or a group of schools over a ten year period. At the higher secondary stage, students were to get experience in the school workshop, or on farms or in the industrial and commercial establishments.

The Commission did recognize the work experience of the basic education. But it pointed out that basic education became largely frozen around certain crafts and highlighted that the society which was to be transformed with the help of science and technology, needed reorientation—work experience had to be forward looking in keeping with the character of the new social order.

(ix) Educational Finance

The Commission considered increasing expenditure on education in the next 20 years from Rs. 12 per capita in 1965-66 to Rs. 54 in 1985-86. The implication was that expenditure which increased from Rs. 1.114 millions in 1950-51 to Rs. 6000 millions in 1985-86 had to rise to Rs. 40364 millions in 1985-86: GDP, allotted to education, had to rise from 2.9% in 1965 to 6.0% in 1985-86. Two thirds of the available resources was to be devoted to school education and one third to higher education.

The main source of educational finance was to be the government, but contributions were to be raised from local communities, voluntary organizations and local authorities. Levying of cess on land revenue was suggested for the *Zila Parishads,* which were to be given grant-in-aid by the State Governments. Similarly, the municipalities were to be given government grants, but these were to be made responsible for supporting at least primary education. The role of the Centre was to assume financial responsibility for education by expanding the central and centrally-sponsored sectors. It was stressed to promote economy consistent with efficiency. It was recommended to conduct research studies on the issues of importance of education for economic growth. The government was to issue a statement on the national policy on education for facilitating implementation plan at State and local levels.

Evaluation

In evaluating the Indian Education Commission Report, the shape of things to come was indicated by Dr. *Kothari's* covering letter to Mr. *Chagla,* the then, Union Minister of Education. The letter reads: "It could have been shorter but that would have cost more money and time and delayed action."

Merits

(*i*) Mr. *Chagla* called it "a unique report".
(*ii*) *The Indian Express,* July 1, 1966 used the words bold and pertinent.
(*iii*) *The Hindustan Times,* July 1, 1966 described the report as a comprehensive, critical and constructive review of the education system prevailing in the country.
(*iv*) *The Hindu,* July 1, 1966 assessed the report in these words—Educationists and teachers welcome the recommendations.
(*v*) *Deccan Chronicle,* July 17, 1966 assessed the report as original and significant contribution.
(*vi*) *Naik* and *Nurullah* called the report a great achievement in the old pursuit of clarifying the concept of a national system of education.
(*vii*) *V.V. John* in *"The Report on Report"* said that the Report "is likely to be on our conscience for a long time to come".

Demerits

(*i*) *M.N. Acharya* in Blitz, 9 July, 1966 criticized the report as a death certificate of basic education.

(*ii*) *The Statesman,* 3 July, 1966 said that the report was sensible in parts but often platitudinous.

(*iii*) *Amrit Bazar Patrika,* 13 July, 1966 dubbed the report as confusing.

Conclusion

Jayaparkash Narayan's foreword is suitable as a conclusion also. He summed up the essence of the report as: pursuit of simultaneous and complementary programmes of social and educational reform, involvement of the entire community in the educational process where the emphasis would have shifted from teaching to learning; co-operation and co-ordination between educational and social-political workers; emphasis on the pursuit of excellence as a way of life; and the primacy of work in the scale of social values.

Yet, it is worth recording that stifling the only attempt at introducing substantially an indigenous scheme of education in the form of basic education by *Gandhiji* is not pardonable. There are diversities in the needs of the learners and those of the society. Thus, both the westernized and indigenous systems of education should have been allowed to make their contribution. The unemployment of the product of the western type of institutions makes us ask: could the craft-centred education not have minimized, if not eliminated, unemployment?

Points to Remember

1. The National Education Commission was appointed in 1964 and it reported in 1966. Its Chairman was Dr. *D.S. Kothari.*
2. The terms of reference were to advise Government on national pattern of education and on the general principles and policies for the development of education at all stages and all its aspects.
3. The recommendations laid down aims of education—economic, political, emotional, social, scientific, and personal.
4. It recommended qualitative improvements and quantitative expansion.
5. Educational pyramid was to be built from pre-primary to the university levels.

6. Professioanl preparation of teachers was considered crucial to the qualitative improvement of ėducation. Salary scales were fixed and improved.
7. Curriculum was laid down from pre-primary to university stages.
8. New teaching methods were to be used.
9. Guidance and counselling were to be the integral part of education.
10. Recommendations were made to ensure equality in educational opportunities between male and female population and between advanced and backward sections of society.
11. Work experience was recommended for students at all levels.
12. The main source of educational finance was to be the Government.
13. The report of the Commission has been lauded, but it has also spelt the doom of basic education.

EXERCISES

1. What recommendations did the National Education Commission, 1964-66 make with relation to aims of education?
2. Comment on the pyramidal structure of education, recommended by the *Kothari* Commission Report.
3. What steps were recommended by the *Kothari* Commission for the improvement of the teaching force?
4. Were the recommendation of the *Kothari* Commission adequate in respect of equalization of educational opportunities?
5. Discuss the financial aspect of the Report of the *Kothari* Commission.
6. What are the merits of the Report of the *Kothari* Commission?
7. How far is it right to say that the *Kothari* Commission sounded the death-knell of basic education?
8. What indications did the *Kothari* Commission Report give about the shape of things to come in the educational world in India?

SECTION–IV

MODERN DEVELOPMENTS
(*FACING REALITIES*)

14

National Policy on Education, 1986

A country like India has ancient traditions of education, almost 5000 years old. Its *Vedic* education recognized that knowledge is 'the third eye'. *Buddhist* education culminated in universities like Taxila and Nalanda. The *maktabs* and *madarasas* kept the literacy tradition going during the medieval times. Christian priests introduced the western type of education in the 1550s. *Raja Rammohun Roy* in the 1830s and *Gopal Krishna Gokhale* in the 1910s knew what the country required, and they worked for it. The western type of education, though meant to produce servile people, sensitized the country to fight for independence. Five year plans—and the importance of education in them—brought us through committees and commissions to a stage at which the Government had no option but to start efforts towards laying down a policy on education. India is a country of surprises and that it took centuries to think of a national policy on education may be acknowledged as one of the surprises.

Need For a Policy

It was the Report of the Education Commission 1964-66 that triggered the thinking faculties of the Government of India. The Report recommended for the Government to issue a statement on the national policy on education with a view to providing guidance to the State Governments and local authorities to prepare and implement educational plans. A committee of the parliament was constituted to prepare a draft which was done and considered by the Central Advisory Board of Education. The outcome was that a resolution on national policy on education was issued in 1968. It aimed at promoting national progress, cultivating a sense of common citizenship and culture and strengthening national integration and pay greater attention to science and technology, moral values, and relate education to the life of the people. It was stipulated to review various programmes on education every five years. Surprisingly, a review was undertaken after 17 years!

A document entitled "Challenge of Education: A Policy Perspective" was prepared and discussed at conferences, seminars and study circles. In addition to English, the document was translated into all the regional languages, Hindi and Urdu, and suggestions were solicited. Finally, the national policy on education was adopted by the *Lok Sabha* and the *Rajya Sabha* in May 1986.

National Policy On Education, 1986

The policy document contains XII Parts and 157 paragraphs on various aspects of education. Part 1 is introductory. Part 2 deals with the essence and role of education. Part 3 dwells on national system of education. Part 4 is concerned with education for equality. Part 5 pertains to reorganization of education at different stages. Part 6 introduces us to technical and management education. Part 7 is entitled as "making the system work". Part 8 highlights the reorienting of the content and process of education. Part 9 is related to the teacher. Part 10 pertains to the management of education. Part 11 is devoted to resources and review. Part 12 talks about the future.

(i) Introductory

The introductory part reviews the progress in education after 1968 and talks of expansion, structural change like 10+2+3, progressive changes in curriculum and progress in post-graduate education and research.

It was, however, realized that "Education in India stands at the cross roads today. Neither normal linear expansion nor the existing pace and nature of improvement can meet the need of the situation."

It was highlighted that in the Indian way of thinking, "a human being is a positive asset and a precious national resource which needs to be cherished, nurtured and developed with tenderness and care, coupled with dynamism. Each individual's growth presents a different range of problems and requirements, at every stage from the womb to the tomb. The catalytic action of education in this complex and dynamic growth process needs to be planned meticulously and executed with great sensitivity."

It was appreciated that a variety of new challenges and social needs make it imperative for the Government to formulate and implement a new education policy for the country. Nothing short of this will meet the situation.

(ii) The Essence and Role of Education

The word "essence" seems to have been used in the sense of "characteristics" and "role" in the sense of "function". Thus, the policy document has the following to say:

(*a*) In our national perception education is essential for all. This is fundamental to our all-round development, material and spiritual.

(*b*) Education has an acculturating role; it refines sensitivities and perceptions that contribute to national cohesion, a scientific temper and independence of mind and spirit—thus furthering the goals of socialism, secularism and democracy, enshrined in our Constitution.

(*c*) Education develops manpower for different levels of the economy. It is also the substrate in which research and development flourish, being the ultimate guarantee of national sefl-reliance.

(*d*) In sum, education is a unique investment in the present and future. This cardinal principle is the key to the National Policy on Education.

A cursory look at the essence and role of education may give the impression that these are mere sentiments, but a thorough examination convinces us that these are realistic and have set the tone not only for the formulation of the policy, but also its implementation.

(iii) National System of Education

The concept of a normal system of education implies that up to a certain level, all students, irrespective of caste, creed, location or sex, have access to education of a comparable quality. The 10+2+3 structure has now been accepted and efforts will be made to breakup first 10 years into 5 years of primary education, 3 years of upper primary, followed by 2 years of high school.

The national system of education will be based on national curricular framework which contains a common core alongwith other components that are flexible. The common core will include the history of India's freedom movement, the constitutional obligation and other content essential to nurture national identity. All educational programmes will be carried on in strict conformity with secular values. Minimum levels of learning will be laid down for each stage of education. Education has to strengthen the world view and motivate the younger generations for international cooperation and peaceful co-existence.

In higher education in general, and technical education in particular, steps will be taken to facilitate inter-regional mobility by providing equal access to every Indian of requisite interest. The universal character of universities and other institutions of higher education is to be underscored. Institutions will pool their resources and participate in projects of national importance.

Lifelong education is a cherished goal of the educational process, which presupposes universal literacy. The future will be in the direction of open and distance learning.

The Constitutional amendment of 1976 has placed education in the concurrent list, but the union government will accept a large responsiblitiy to reinforce the national and integrative character of education and maintain quality and standards: promote excellence at all levels of the educational pyramid throughout the country.

(iv) Education for Equality

The new policy will lay special emphasis on the removal of disparities and to equalize educational opportunity by attending to the specific need of those who have been denied equality so far. The targets are:

(*a*) Women (*b*) Scheduled Castes, (*c*) Scheduled Tribes (*d*) Other backward section and areas, (*e*) Minorities (*f*) Handicapped, (*g*) Illiterate adults.

(a) Education for Women's Equality

The national education system will play positive interventionist role in the empowerment of women. It will foster the development of new values through redesigned curricula, text books, the training and orientation of teachers, decision-makers and administrators and active involvement of educational institutions. The overriding priority will be the retention of women in elementary and professional education at different levels. The sex stereotyping in vocational and professional courses will be eliminated.

(b) Education of Schedule Castes

Incentives will be provided to indigent families to send their children to school regularly till they reach the age of 14. Pre-matric scholarship scheme is envisaged for children of scavengers and those engaged in flaying and tanning occupations. Provisions of remedial courses are to be made to encourage SC children for further education and employment. Teachers from the SC are to be recruited. Facilities like buildings, *balwadis* and adult education centres should be extended to the SC.

(c) Education of the Schedule Tribes

Priority will be accorded to opening primary schools in tribal areas. Initially, the curricula will be developed in the tribal language; later on, regional language will be used. Young people from the ST should be trained to take up teaching in tribal areas. Scholarships for higher education will emphasise technical, professional and para-professional courses. *Anganwadis*, non-formal and adult education centres will be opened on priority basis.

(d) Education of the Backward Section

Hill and desert districts, remote and inaccessible areas and islands will be provided adequate institutional infrastructure.

(e) Education of the Minorities

Minorities, as per the constitutional guarantees, should establish and administer their languages and institutions and protect their languages and culture. Objectivity will be reflected in the preparation of text books and in all school activities. All possible measures will be taken to promote an integration based on appreciation of common goals and ideals in conformity with the core curriculum.

(f) Education of the Handicapped

The objective should be to integrate the physically and mentally handicapped with the general community as equal partners. Thus, the education of children with motor and other minor handicapped will be common with that of others. Special schools with hostels will be provided for severely handicapped children. Vocational training will be arranged and teachers reoriented to deal with special difficulties of the handicapped children.

(g) Adult Education

Provision to make adults read and write should be linked with national goals and acquisition of skills. Centres for continuing education should be established in rural areas and workers education should be undertaken by employers, trade unions etc. Books and literacy and reading rooms should be promoted and mass-media used. Programmes of distance learning should be developed.

(v) Reorganisation of Education

Reorganisation of education starts with early childhood care and education, passes through the elementary stages to second level of education and then to universities. It also includes vocationalisation of education.

(a) Early Childhood Care and Education (ECCE)

The NPE recognises the holistic nature of child development, viz., nutrition, health, social, mental, physcial, moral and emotional development and accords ECCE a high priority. It will be integrated with the child development services programme. Day-care centres will be provided.

The programme of ECCE will be child-oriented. The focus will be on play and individuality of the child. The programmes will be both as a feeder and a strengthening factor for primary education and for human resource development in general.

(b) Elementary Education

The new thrust in elmentary education will emphasise universal enrolement and retention of children upto 14 years of age, and a substantial improvement in the quality of education. A child-centred and activity-based process of learning should be adopted. The policy of non-detention will be retained. Corporal punishment will be formally excluded from the system. In so far as school timings and vacations are concerned, these will be adjusted to the convenience of children. Operation blackboard will include school facilities—reasonably large rooms, toys, blackboards, maps, charts and other learning materials. Non-formal education will be launched for school drop outs, children whose habitations have no schools and also for those who cannot attend whole-day schools. The NPE centres will use modern technological aids and provide participatory learning environment. The NPE envisages that by 1995 all children will be provided education up to 14 years of age.

(c) Secondary Education

The NPE recognises the role of secondary education when it begins to expose students to the differentiated role of science, humanities and social sciences. At this stage, children should be provided with a sense of history and national perspective and given opportunities to understand the constitutional duties and rights as citizens. The curricula will bring about conscious internalisation of a healthy work ethos and of the values of human and composite culture.

Pace-setting schools *'Navodya Vidyalaya'* will be established for children with special talent or aptitude. The objective will be to serve excellence but with reservations for SC and ST in that principles of equality and social justice will also be met.

(d) Vocationalisation

Vocational education will be a distinct stream to prepare students for identified occupations, spreading several areas of activity, provided after secondary stage or class VIII.

(e) University education

The open university system has been initiated in order to augment opportunities for higher education. The Indira Gandhi National Open University will be strengthened. Degrees, except for occupation-specific disciplines like engineering, medicine, law, teaching etc., will be delinked from jobs. A new pattern of rural university will be consolidated and developed.

(vi) Technical and Management Education

The reorganisation of technical and management education should take into account the likely changes by the turn of the century in the economy, social environment, production and management processes, the rapid expansion of knowledge and the great advances in science and technology. In the field of manpower information, the technical manpower information system will be further developed and strengthened.

Higher technical institutions will undertake renovation and renewal of education through research. Efficiency and effectiveness will be promoted at all levels by means of modernisation, generating resources, improving the lot of teachers, targeting the curriculum on the needs of the industry and promoting excellence. Commercialisation of technical and professional education will be curbed.

(vii) Making the System Work

Education needs to be managed in an atmosphere of utmost intellectual vigour, seriousness of purpose and of freedom essential for innovation and creativity. To make the system work, all teachers should teach and all students study. The strategy will consist of a better deal to teachers with greater accountability, provision of improved student services, insistence on observance of acceptable norms of behaviour, better facilities to institutions and creation of a system of performance appraisal of institutions, following the norms set at the national or State levels.

(viii) The Content and Process of Education

The curricula and processes of education will be enriched by cultural content: children will be enabled to develop sensitivity to beauty, harmony and refinement. Linkages will be established between the university system and institutions of higher learning in art, archaeology, oriental studies etc. Due attention will also be paid to fine art, musicology, folklore etc.

In our culturally plural society, education should foster universal and eternal values, oriented towards the unity and integrity of our people. Value education should help elimination of obscurantism, religious fanaticism, violence, superstition and fatalism.

The policy on the development of languages will be implemeted more energetically. Good translations of foreign books into Indian languages will be supported. Measures will be taken to improve the quality of books. Education technology will be employed in the spread of useful information. The generation of relevant and culturally compatible educational programmes will form important components of education technology. Radio and T.V. programmes which clearly militate against proper educational objectives will be prevented.

Work experience, viewed as purposive and meaningful manual work, organised as an integral part of the learning process and resulting in either goods or services useful to the community, is considered as an essential component at all stages of education. It is to be provided through well structured and graded programmes. Environmental consciousness will be integrated in the entire educational process.

Teaching of mathematics should be treated as means to enable a child to think, reason, analyse and articulate logically. With the help of computers, mathematics will be suitably redesigned to bring it in line with modern technological devices. Science education should develop spirit of inquiry, creativity, objectivity, the courage to question and an aesthetic sensibility. A nationwide infrastructure for physical education, sports and games will be built into the educational edifice and efforts made to introduce *yoga* in all schools. Students should participate in the National Service Scheme, National Cadet Corps etc.

Evaluation process through examination should eliminate the excessive element of chance and subjectivity; continuous and comprehensive evaluation should be spread over the total span of instructional time. Semester system and use of grades in place of marks should be introduced.

(ix) The Teacher

The policy recognises that the status of the teacher reflects the socio-cultural ethos of a society. The government and the community should endeavour to create conditions which will help motivate and inspire teachers on constructive and creative lines. The method of recruitment will be reorganised to ensure merit, objectivity and conformity with spatial and functional requirements. The pay and service conditions of teachers have to be in commensurate with their social and professional responsibilities and with the need to attract talent to the profession. The new programmes of teacher education will emphasise continuing education. District Institutes of Education and Training will be established with the capability to organise pre-service and in-service courses. The National Council for Teacher Education will be provided the necessary resources and capability to accredit institutions of teacher education and provide guidance regarding curricula and methods.

(x) The Management of Education

In the management of education, it was recommended to evolve a long term planning and management perspective of education and its integration with the country's developmental and manpower needs. Decentralisation of education and creating a spirit of autonomy for educational institutions, with people's involvement including women—in education planning and management was recommended. Establishment of principle of accountability in relation to given objectives and norms is also recommended. The Central Advisory Board of Education will play a pivotal role in reviewing educational development. Bodies like Indian Education Service, State and local level advisory boards will manage education at various levels.

(xi) Resources and Review

It has been stressed in various reports that the egalitarian goals and the practical development-oriented objectives of Indian society can be realised only by making investment in education of an order commensurate with the nature and dimension of the task. Donations, maintaining buildings by the communities, levying a cess etc. will be mobilised. The policy considered its review every five years, although appraisal of various parameters will be done at short intervals to ascertain progress.

(xii) The Future

The main task is to strengthen the base of the pyramid. But, it is important to ensure that those at the top of the pyramid are among the best in the world. It should be possible to further intensity the nation-wide effort in human resource development, with education playing its multifaceted role.

Evaluation

To evaluate a document of the dimensions, outlined in the NPE 1986, is not an easy task. Yet, there is hardly any document, which is definitive in concept and practice: all human efforts lend themselves to evaluation, so is the case with the Policy document of 1986.

Merits

(*i*) After its publication is 1986, Mr. *R.K. Trivedi*, then the Governor of Gujarat, said that "considering the all round development of the country the structure of Education Policy was erected. Education is not considered within the four walls of the schools. Teaching is not limited to the curriculum but it is a source of developing national unity, cultural preservation and inculcation of moral, social and ethical values."

(*ii*) The role of education is stated in comprehensive terms as all round development and acculturation. Stress is laid on the human resource devlopment.

(*iii*) The national structure of education is provided in the shape of 10+2+3.

(*iv*) Equalisation of educational opportunities is stated in clearer terms.

(*v*) Provisions are made for the education of women, scheduled castes and other backward classes.

(*vi*) The problem of adult illiteracy is addressed through traditional and innovative programmes like distance education.

(*vii*) The blueprint of education pyramid is clearly stated.

Limitations

(*i*) The explosion in population will not make it easy to cope with the formulations of the Policy document.

(*ii*) On the one hand, the *Navodaya Vidyalaya* faced infrastructural and teaching force problems, on the other, they have turned out to be "public" schools like those in England—but here, these are State financed.

(*iii*) The expectations from the community are rather too high.

(*iv*) Too much of reservation for different categories of population has tended to stifle talent.

(*v*) There is no check on the working of the minority institutions.

(*vi*) The guidelines for the future are somewhat hazy.

Conclusion

After the announcement of the Policy, Programme of Action for its implementation was also declared by the Ministry of

Human Resource Development in the main areas like national system of education, reconstruction of curriculum, operation blackboard, *Navodaya Vidyalayas* and vocationalisation.

The Policy had stipulated revision in every five years. Such revision did take place in 1992, showing the dynamic nature of the document. It seems that the late Prime Minister *Rajeev Gandhi*'s words that in our society "education must be honoured" have been honoured by the revision and may also be honoured in the future.

Points to Remember

1. National Policy on Education was adopted in 1986.
2. It defines the comprehensive role of education.
3. The 10+2+3 structure of education is provided.
4. The Policy provides equal opportunities for education for all.
5. It takes care of education of women, schedule castes, other backward classes and illiterate adults.
6. It has built an educational pyramid.
7. New dimensions like distance education through the open universities are added.
8. The overall impact of the Policy is positive although too much reservation for SCs and STs may stifle the talent.

EXERCISES

1. Examine the background to the adoption of National Policy on Education, 1986.
2. Comment on the desirability or otherwise of 10+2+3 structure of education.
3. Discuss the statement that NPE, 1986 is a boon to our country.
4. How does the NPE, 1986 provide for equalisation of educational opportunities?
5. What measures are suggested in the NPE, 1986 to eradicate illiteracy?
6. What steps have been taken in the NPE, 1986 to improve the teaching force.
7. Comment on the following statement:
   "The NPE, 1986 has so many positive aspects that its limitations are not easy to identify"—Authors.

15

Revised National Policy on Education and Programme of Action, 1992

The revision of NPE, 1986 and of the POA were partly the result of the stipulation to effect revisions after 5 years and partly the change of guard in the government. The Janta Dal government was somewhat lukewarm to the NPE, formulated by the Congress government. Thus, a review committee under *Acharya Rammurti* as Chairman was appointed in 1990. Its report was placed in 1991 before the CABE which appointed another committee under *Janardhana Reddy* as Chairman to reconsider the recommendations of the *Rammurti Committee* and also examine the NPE. The *Reddy* Committee submitted its report in 1992. Furthermore, the *Yaspal* Committee, 1992-93 suggested modifications in the POA.

Rammurti Committee

The Committee had *Acharya Rammurti* as Chairman and 16 other members.

Terms of Reference

The Committee was given the following terms of reference:

(*a*) Review of National Policy on Education, 1986 and its application.

(*b*) Suggestions for implementation concerning the NPE.

(*c*) Suggestions for implementation of revised policy. Determination of the terms of reference of right of employment, national integrity and diminishing human values. The Committee submitted its report in 15 chapters.

Modus Operandi

The Committee issued a Perspective Paper on Education in September 1990 and sought response before 10th October. Three basic concerns were highlighted—(*a*) the right to work which is proposed to be enshrined in the Constitution. (*b*) the unity and integrity of the nation are seriously threatened and (*c*) the impoverishment of the men in India. There is a point of view that the paper is directed towards an enlightened and human society.

Main Aspects of the Review

The review starts with early childhood care education, and deals with adult education, right of jobs, higher education, education complex and resources for education etc.

(a) Early Childhood Care Education (ECCE)

The Committee suggested that ECCE centres be established near primary schools. The curriculum for classes 1-3 should be included in teacher training. Para schools should be opened and attached to primary schools. Girls should be provided with text books, scholarships, school dress, hostel facilities etc., and complaints of sexual harassment should be taken seriously. Regional disparities should be eradicated. Common school system should be developed. No new *Navodaya Schools* should be opened, but the existing ones should be well equipped.

(b) Universalisation of Primary Education

The ECCE centres should be looked after with the help of the *anganwadis*. Non-graded system should be followed and cooperative teachers, appointed by the Head Master, should get half or one-third of the schools salary and work on probation for three years.

(c) Adult Education

Follow up education is suggested. Model for it is to be proposed by the literacy mission. Constitutional mandate of free and compulsory education up to age of 14 has been looked into.

(d) Right of jobs

It was suggested that every educated person has a right of job. A link should be established between the world of school and world of work.

(e) Higher Education

The development of higher education should follow the system of the UGC. Degree should be delinked from the jobs. The rural universities should come under the State Higher Education Councils.

(f) Education Complex

Education complex comprises local colleges, secondary and middle schools, governed by local bodies. They should enjoy functional autonomy.

(g) Resources for Education

Strategies for augmenting resources for education and distribution of the same were outlined. The eighth finance commission has accepted education as a non-development area and urged for its progress on the basis of physical norms.

(iv) Evaluation

The *Rammurti Committee* saved itself from being dubbed as a formality because it made important suggestions. It focused on the controversial and non-beneficial *Navodaya Schools* and increasing use of English. That the report made the government review it and also the NPE, 1986 show that it was not ignored.

Janardhan Reddy Committee

The Committee was constituted on the direction of the CABE under the Chairmanship of *Janardhan Reddy*, the then, Chief Minister of Andhra Pradesh. The membership comprised political parties and eight educationists. It was to reconsider the *Rammurti Committee* Report and review the original document of NPE, 1986.

Modus Operandi

The Committee constituted twenty-two task forces on different aspects of education. The task forces comprised educationists and officials of Union and State Governments. The task forces reformulated programme of action, presented the draft to CABE, which endorsed it and the Government accepted it.

Main Themes

The major themes relate to various aspects of education outlined in the NPE, 1986 and the POA.

Revised Policy and Programme of Action, 1992

(*i*) *National System of Education*: The 10+2+3 educational structure was accepted. The break of first ten years into (*a*) five years primary education (*b*) three years upper primary and (*c*) two years of high school was suggested.

(*ii*) *Education for Women's Equality*: Education for women's equality was considered a vital component of the overall strategy of securing equity and social justice, as according to 1991 Census, female literacy rate was 39.41 percent compared to 63.86 percent for males. Universal elementary education was impossible unless girl child was educated. There were to be improvement of girl's access to technical, vocational and professional education. Management structure was to be outlined at Centre and State levels for curriculum development, training and research.

(*iii*) *Education for SCs/STs and OBCs*: Universal access to education was to be ensured and adequate incentives were to be given to children, particularly the girls. Schools were to be equipped with facilities. Reservations were to be made. Operation blackboard was to cover all schools in tribal areas and *Harijan bastis*.

(*iv*) *Minorities Education*: NCERT was to make training programmes for principals, managers and teachers of minorities. Remedial coaching schemes, scholarships and incentives were to be undertaken on short, medium and long-term basis.

(*v*) *Education of the Handicapped*: Provisions like integrated education for disabled children, establishment of special schools for severe cases, vocational training, orientation and training of regular teachers, recruitment of special teachers, educational and vocational guidance, use of mass media and Braille were suggested.

(*vi*) *Early Childhood Care and Education*: There was to be adequate number of workers in *balwadis*, day care centres, pre-primary schools, maternal and child health service.

(*vii*) *Elementary Education*: Non-formal education was to be accepted as an alternative channel. Education for all was to be encouraged. 50 percent of teachers was to be of women. Load of school bag and academic burden were to be decreased.

(*viii*) *Secondary Education:* 10+2+3 structure was suggested. Qualitative improvement, modernization of curriculum and evaluation of text books were suggested.

(*ix*) *Navodaya Vidyalayas*: All districts were to be covered by the end of the 8th plan. 50 *Vidyalayas* were to be opened every year at minimum costs. Talented teachers were to be recruited and the institutions were to be accountable to the community.

(*x*) *Higher Education*: The main features of the higher education were to impart dynamism by consolidation and expansion of institutions giving autonomy to colleges and departments, redesigning of courses, training of teachers, strengthening research and improving efficiency and coordination at the States and national levels. Accreditation and assessment machinery was to be set up. Each State was to establish an Open University. Degrees were to be delinked from jobs in selected areas. The Central Council of Rural Institutes was expected to be set up shortly.

(*xi*) *Technical and Management Education*: In technical and management education, the important topics discussed were: schemes of continuing education, industry-institute interaction, management development programme, curriculum development, modernization of technical education, review of IIMs and IITs, reviews of community polytechnics, All India Council for Technical Education, P.G. Education, Management Education etc.

(*xii*) *Research and Development*: Main problems and shortcomings, linkages and monitoring of programmes were discussed.

(*xiii*) *The Cultural Perspective*: For pre-primary stage, a cultural primer was to be prepared. For children of primary stage, children theatre school movement was to be launched. For middle or secondary stage, India's natural and cultural heritage were to be taught and competition of school magazines organized. Cultural exposures were to be enlarged. At the university level, cultural courses like music, fine arts, performing arts, and courses in translation etc. were to be undertaken.

(*xiv*) *Development of Languages:* The three-language formula was discussed. A certain level of language competency to be achieved might be determined. About 1000 Hindi teachers were to be appointed in 8th Plan with central assistance. In pursuance to Article 350 of the Constitution, Union of India was to promote, develop and propagate Hindi. The Committee proposed to strengthen *Rashtriya Sanskrit Sansthan, Rashtriya Ved Vidya Pratishthan* and to open new *Kendrya Sanskrit Vidyapeeths.*

(*xv*) *Sports, Physical Education and Youth*: Physical education and *yoga* were to be introduced for at least 45 minutes per day. Special incentives were to be provided to promote *yoga*, sports and games. Service of *Nehru Yuva Kendras*, NSS, *Bharat Scouts and Guides* and NCC were to be expanded.

(*xvi*) *Teacher Education*: Centrally-sponsored scheme of teacher education was suggested and special orientation for school teachers was also envisaged. Establishing and strengthening of departments of education in the universities, and accountability of teachers were suggested.

(*xvii*) *Management and Education*: Management of education was discussed and it was to be under *panchayati raj* bodies, district level body, and village committee, urban local bodies, NGOs etc. A process was to be worked out for establishing Indian Education Service. Accountability and efficiency were discussed.

The programme of action, 1992 could be implemented only if the Union and States/Union Territories and the education community worked cooperatively. But the approach to implementation was to be flexible in face of the diversity in the country vis-a-vis the resources. The POA acknowledged the usefulness of many salient features of the Policy document of 1986 and the *Rammurti* Commitee Report of 1990 and made suggestions to expand *Navodaya Vidyalayas.*

The *Yashpal* Committee, 1992-93

The *Yashpal* Committee was established to examine the POA, 1992 which had observed that "the tendency on the part of some schools, particularly in urban areas, to recommend a large number of books, had contributed to overburdening of students." The criticism of M.Ps. like R.K. Narayan in the Parliament and by the mass media regarding overburdening of students with the books was taken note of. The Committee was to advise on the ways and means to reduce the burden of the school child. The Committee made valuable observations and recommendations. The main recommendations were:

(i) Curriculum

The processes of curriculum framing and preparation of textbooks were to be decentralized to district-level boards. There was to be greater involvement of teachers in related activities. Voluntary organizations were to be provided greater freedom and support for curriculum, textbooks and teacher training. A project team was to be set up in each State with sub groups to decide on the minimum number of topics/minimum concepts to be taught and the time needed for each exercise.

A review of mathematics curriculum of primary stage was recommended to encourage space-related concepts and problem solving, understanding and independent applications. Language textbooks were to adequately reflect spoken idiom and also focus on children's life experience and stories reflecting the lives of ordinary people. A great deal of trivial material in primary level science texts was to be dropped. Revision of natural science syllabi for secondary/senior secondary classes was to link topics with experiments or activities by children and teachers. Social science curriculum for classes 6 to 10 was to focus on socio-political and economic systems. History of ancient times was to be introduced in secondary classes; history syllabus for classes 6 to 8 was to focus on the freedom struggle and post-independence developments. Civics was to be replaced by contemporary studies, and the study of geography was to be related to contemporary reality. Experts were to be consultants and not writers of textbooks. Greater use was to be made of the electronic media for creation of a child-centred social ethos. Individual competitions and awards were to be discouraged and group activities/achivements were to be encouraged and rewarded.

No homework was to be assigned at the primary stage. Homework in upper primary and secondary stages was to be non-textual and textbooks—the property of the school—were to be issued for homework on rotational basis. The public examinations at class 10 and class 12 levels were to be reviewed and text-based-quiz-type questions replaced by concept-based questions.

(ii) Administration

Education committees at village, block and district levels were to be set up to undertake planning and supervision of schools. A contingency amount (not less than 10% of salary bill) was to be placed at the disposed of heads of schools for purchase, repair and replacement of pedagogical equipment. CBSE affiliation was to be restricted to Kendriya Vidyalayas and Navodaya Vidyalayas only. Appropriate legislative/administrative measures were to be adopted to regulate opening and functioning of pre-schools. Test-interviews for admission were to be abolished. Norms for granting recognition to private schools were be made more stringent. It was recommended to enforce the existing teacher-pupil ratio at 1:40 and to make an attempt to reduce this to 1:30, at least in primary classes.

(ii) Teacher Training

B.Ed. degree courses by correspondence were recommended to be de-recognized. B.Ed. programme was to offer specialization in secondary, elementary and nursery education. The content was to be practical-centred.

Task Before a Group

To examine the feasibility of implementing the recommendations of the *Yaspal* Committee, the Ministry of HRD appointed a group under the Chairmanship of *Y.N. Chaturavedi*, Additional Secretary, Department of Education, Government of India "to advise on the ways and means to reduce the load of books on school students at all levels, particularly the young students, while improving quality of learning including capability for lifelong self-learning and skill formulation".

Conclusion

Over the years, through the work of commissions, we were able to bring about a policy on education. Its implementation was carried out by means of the programme of action. The programme was evaluated by three committees. Ultimately a "group" was formed to study the ways and means to reduce the load of books and work on the students. Situation could be interpreted as an anti-climax because so much was delivered quantitatively and qualitatively by the high-powered commissions and committees and by the comprehensive policy on education that a "group" appears to be a dwarf before the giants.

Points to Remember

1. What led to the National Policy on Education and policy itself were the efforts of the Congress governments. When Janata Dal Government came to power, it appointed a review committee under the Chairmanship of *Rammurti*. It reported in 1990.
2. The *Rammurti* Committee Report addressed itself to early childhood care and education and suggested to established such schools near the primary schools. *Angnawadis* were to help the ECCE. No new *Navodaya Schools* were to be opened. Degrees were to be de-linked from the jobs. Every educated person had a right to work.
3. The *Reddy* Committee was constituted to reconsider the recommendations of the *Rammurti* Committee. It reported in 1992.
4. The Committee accepted the 10+2+3 structure, but suggested division of first years into 5 years primary, 3 years upper primary and 2 years of high school.
5. It considered education from women's equality as social justice and recommended universal primary education and access to technical, vocational and professional education for women.
6. Recommendations were made for incentives to SCs, STs and OBCs and different provisions for the handicapped.
7. All districts were to be covered with the *Navodaya Vidyalayas*.
8. Autonomy was stressed in higher institutions of learning.

9. Modernization of technical education was suggested.
10. The three language formula was discussed.
11. There was to be decentralization of management of education.
12. The *Yashpal* Committee suggested ways to reduce the burden of books on the children.
13. A group reviewed the recommendations of the *Yaspal* Committee.

EXERCISES

1. Examine the need for the setting up of the *Rammurti* Committee in 1990.
2. What suggestions did the *Rammurti* Committee make in relation to early childhood care and education?
3. Discuss the recommendations of the *Reddy* Committee on the issue of education for the women's equality.
4. What did the *Reddy* Committee say about higher education?
5. Comment on the recommendations of the *Yaspal* Committee.
6. Elaborate the following statement:
   "The group constituted by the HRD Ministry to examine the feasibility of implementing the *Yashpal* Committee report was an anti-climax to the developments set in motion since 1986"—Authors.

16

Development of Educational System in India: A Critique

In the history of development of educational system in India, different trends have been observed. Generally, the interacting, interrelated and interdependent elements—the constituents of a system—have not quite formed a collective entity any time. For example, the *Vedic*, the *Buddhist*, the Muslim and the Christian educational systems were dominated by spiritual considerations. The western type of education during the colonial period aimed at the production of people with the servile mental make up. After independence, there have been idealistic formulations in the Constitution, in the reports of committees and commissions and in the policies of governments, but the programmes of action and their impact have not been quite able to meet the intentions of the formulations. The reasons behind the state of affairs in the present system of education at various levels are philosophical, social, political, economic and administrative. However, it is not easy to separate these elements into watertight compartments: these are interrelated.

Philosophical Positions

The western type of education in India has continued with the western schools of philosophy and the dominant note in such schools has been the British type which was a compromise between the Roman Catholic and the Protestant philosophies of education: the former being somewhat rigid on "idealism" and the latter inclining towards "realism". Except for the *Gandhian* philosophy of education, little appears to be forthcoming as an attempt at evolving an indigenous philosophy of education until the National Policy on Education, 1986.

The 1986 policy lacks in any clear cut philosophical positions, which can be adjudged to be indigenous. At best, the policy document is eclectic in nature. In addition to the philosophical inputs of traditional philosophical schools of education in the western world—naturalism, idealism, realism, pragmatism—one can identify views of Indian thinkers like *Guru Nanak, Vivekananda, Dayananda, Gandhi* and *Tagore.*

In aims of education, institutions of learning, status of pupils, role of teachers and curriculum, it is easy to identify eclectic trends. The problems with eclecticism as a philosophy of education in India after the policy of 1986 is the lack of what *Paul Munroe* calls the harmonization of principles underlying various tendencies and rationalization of educational practices. Let us examine the provisions of education at various levels.

(i) Pre-Primary Education

The NPE, 1986 uses the term "Early Childhood Care and Education" (ECCE) for nursery, kindergarten and *Montensori* type of schools. Nearly, a decade has passed, yet no large scale programmes have been mounted by the governments—Congress or BJP or others. The pre-primary education is still in the care of private enterprise, which runs schools and centres in the traditional and commercial ways. The Policy advocates that the base of the educational pyramid should be pre-primary education. But the question arises: how many day-care centres are there for the children of the working mothers? There are, perhaps, more working mothers on the farms, in the factories and in the construction enterprises than in the offices. Furthermore, how is the pre-primary education interrelating with primary education? Is it interrelating at all as the State provisions are negligible. Does not a system mean interrelation?

(ii) Primary Education

Universal elementary education has been made a fundamental right since 2002. The *Sarva Shiksha Abhiyan* at the elementary stage expects all children to complete five years of primary schooling by 2007, but it proved as a great failure as still dropouts rate is very high. The Tenth Five Years Plan envisages universal access, universal retention and universal achievement. Is it possible to achieve these objectives within a year or so of the plan period? If the catchment areas—the pre-primary schools—are yet to broaden the base, how can the element of interdependence, an essential ingredient to a "system", be justified? Are the product of primary schools academically sound enough to benefit from education at the secondary level?

(iii) Secondary Education

Assuming that the entrants to secondary schools are reasonably "educated" at the primary level, they still face a number of problems. They find that the curriculum is single track: they have no choice in selecting subjects which are according to their needs, desires and interests. They also find that the school climate is not all that conducive to learning. There is indiscipline, the standard of teaching is low as some teachers make teaching a one-way traffic and do not motivate learners to discover knowledge on their own. Perhaps, the students are prepared sufficiently to go for higher education, but find it difficult to enter the job market or be self-employed for lack of skills and competencies: is not vocationalization at the secondary school level merely a label? Secondary education system totally fails to instil creativity in learness and produces unskilled manpower. Secondary Education turns out those who are just like unguided missiles: they donot know where to go and what to do?

(iv) Higher Education

The opportunities for higher education have been provided by countries according to their needs. In the USA, all have the opportunity to run the race, but very few reach the line. In the UK, the process is selective at various levels. In India, it is merit-based except for the SCs/STs and OBCs. Universalisation of primary education will mean more students at the secondary level and more entrants to the universities. Even with the present provisions of higher education, there is educated unemployment. Falling standards are noticeable; student indiscipline is rampant; poor infrastructural facilities are encountered; and there is lack of finance. Do two maladies not inflict the university system: political interference and erosion of autonomy?

Have our universities been achieving excellence and providing knowledge useful for future life as Lord *Robins* expected in England? Do the universities stand for humansim, as was the wish of *Jawahar Lal Nehru*? Do they give birth of great personalities as was recommended by the *Radhakrishnan* Commission? Have the universities been able to develop proper understanding of self and the world, as was the view of the *Kothari* Commission? Are the stipulations of national policy on education that higher education provides people with an opportunity to reflect on the critical social, economic, moral and spiritual issues facing humanity being met? Will not answers to these questions enable us to determine whether or not the universities in India have a right to be at the apex of the educational pyramid–educational system?

Social Issues

The social issues relate to the contribution of the educational sector to the amelioration of conditions of the poor lot of our people. Though educated manpower does provide services in various fields of life, only health and transport seem to be of direct benefit to the ordinary people. Many educated people look down upon the poor, even though some of them might have risen from the poor background. There is an anecdote about a woman deputy in the former Supreme Soviet who was once a tractor driver and an American who rose from rags to riches. When the deputy was asked about the difference, she said that the person in America had risen from his people: she had risen with her people. How soon are we going to reach the stage when we will be able to say what the woman deputy had said? Social distance between the 'high' and 'low' need narrowing down, but should it be done at the cost of talent?

Political Scenario

By and large, politics in India is now a career and not a service. There are some who are sincerely committed to serve the people, but they are an exception. Large majority of the political class wants to earn money, fairly or otherwise. Although politicians differ on the basis of region, religion, caste, political creed etc., yet for getting rich, many are comrades-in-arms. The politics in India is full of nepotism, casteism, regionalism, jingoism, opportunitism and any other "isms", except for "patriotism" in many cases. The false promises before elections and stiff neck when they are in power seem to be the fashion of the political class in general. Does not a 'system' require cleanliness for it to function productively?

Economic Considerations

It is true that financial input into the educational sector has been on the increase. But it has not caught up with the increase in student population. More and better institutions at all levels, manned by qualified teachers, call for more finances. The policy document of 1986 does label expenditure on education as an investment in human resource development. Is the investment adequate? Is it being spent judiciously? Is there equitable provision for funds? Does not an educational system worth its name require sufficient financial outlay?

Administrative Situation

Administratively, are we staffing the educational enterprise with people, suitable enough in the areas of technical, human and conceptual skills? We call head teachers, principals, heads of the departments and vice-chancellors as leaders. Are they leaders indeed? A leader is an innovative person. How much scope is there for creativity and innovation in a system of education which is hierarchical and is remote-controlled by politicians—a mixed bag of semi-literate and educated lots?

Conclusion

In the previous chapters, we have traced the developmental processes, examined problems and identified prospects for the development of educational system in India. We have reached a stage in the development at which we can discern more theoretical stipulations which appeal to our heart. What we need is to make the system work and plan for more development in the future. Such efforts require congnitive and pragmatic approaches in addition to the affective approach. When a system develops and grows, it cannot afford to neglect the interrelationship and interdependence of its components—vertically and horizontally.

Select Bibliography

Books

Aggarwal, J.C. (2004). *Development of Education System in India*, Shipra Publications, Delhi.

Attekar, A.S. (1974). *Education in Ancient India*, Motilal Banarasi Dass, Varanasi.

Bhatnagar, Suresh (2004). *Education in India*, International Publishing House, Meerut.

Bhatnagar, Suresh et. al. (2002) *Development of Education System in India*, R. Lall Book Depot, Meerut.

Kundu, C.L. (1979). *India Yearbook on Teacher Education*, Sterling Publishers, New Delhi.

Mathur V.S. (1968). *Studies is Indian Education*, Arya Book Depot, New Delhi.

Mukherjee, R.K. (1980). *Education in India, Today and Tomorrow*, Achaarya Book Depot, Baroda,

Nurullah Syed and Naik, J.P. (1955). *A Student History of Education*, MacMillan Co., India Ltd. Bombay.

Rajput, J.S. (1999). *Education in a Changing World*: Practices and Forces, Vikas Publishing House, New Delhi.

Rawat, P.L. (1968). *History of Indian Education*, Ram Prasad & Sons, Agra.

Saiyidain, K.G. (1965). *Education: Science of Education*, Raj Kamal Prakashan, New Delhi.

Sharma, R.A. (2004). *Development of Educational System*. Surya Publication, Meerut.

Srivastava, R.C. (1973). *Theory and Practice of Teacher Education in India*, Chug Publication, Allahabad.

Reports: Government of India

The Constitution of India, 1950

Report of University Education Commission: The *Radhakrishanan* Commission, 1949.

Report of Secondary Education Commission, the *Mudaliar* Commision, 1953.
Report of Indian Education Commission, the *Kothari* Commission, 1966.
National Policy on Education, 1986.
Programme of Action: National Policy on Education, 1992.

Relevant Documents

1835-38	*William Adams*: Three Reports on Education.
1835	Lord *Maculay's* Minute
1835	*Bentinck's* Resolution
1854	*Wood's* Despatch
1882	The *Hunter* Commission
1901	Simla Educational Conference
1902	Indian Universities Commission
1904	Indian Universities Act
1906	National Education Movement
1911	*Gokhale's* Bill
1917	The *Sadler* Commission
1929	The *Hartog* Committee
1935	Government of India Act
1936-37	*Abbot-Wood* Report
1937	The *Zakir Hussain* Committee: Wardha Scheme of Education
1944	The Sargent Report
1950	The *Kher* Committee
1956	The University Grants Commission Act
1960	The *Sri Prakasha* Committee
1966	The *Saiyidan* Committee
1986	National Policy on Education
1987	The *Mehrotra* Committee
1990	The *Rammurti* Committee
1992	The *Reddy* Committee
1992-93	The *Yashpal* Committee
1993	National Council for Teacher Education Act
2000	*Ambani-Birla* Committee.

Journals

NIE Journal, National Council of Educational Research and Training, New Delhi, September-November, 1966.
Journal of Higher Education. Vol. 8. No. 1. University Grants Commission, New Delhi, 1982.
University News, Special Issue December, 18-19 1987. Association of Indian Universities, New Delhi.
The Progress of Education, Vol. 58. No. 4 November, 1993, Vidyarthi Grih Prakashan, Pune.